E 6
ART
1918

New Asian Style

New Asian Style

Contemporary Tropical Living in Singapore

Jane Doughty Marsden

Photography by Masano Kawana

PERIPLUS

Published by Periplus Editions (HK) Ltd

Copyright © 2002 Periplus Editions (HK) Ltd
Text © 2002 Jane Doughty Marsden
Photos © 2002 Masano Kawana

ISBN 962-593-827-3

Printed in Singapore
Editors: Kim Inglis, Jocelyn Lau
Design: mind, London
Photographic coordinator: Yaeko Masuda

Distributed by:
North America
Tuttle Publishing, Distribution Center,
Airport Industrial Park, 364 Innovation Drive, North
Clarendon, VT 05759-9436, USA
Tel (802) 773 8930; fax (802) 773 6993

Asia Pacific
Berkeley Books Pte Ltd, 130 Joo Seng Road,
#06-01/03, Olivine Building, Singapore 368357,
Republic of Singapore
Tel (65) 280 3320; fax (65) 280 6290

Japan and Korea
Tuttle Publishing, RK Building, 2nd Floor,
2-13-10 Shimo-Meguro, Meguro-Ku,
Tokyo 153, Japan
Tel (813) 5437 0171; fax (813) 5437 0755

Cover: Burmese *balau* and two antique water
jars provide the only strong colours in a
minimalist house designed by Chan Soo Khian
of SCDA. *Title page: Chenggal* louvres and
low seating arrangement at the Lees' SCDA
Architects' designed home. *Previous pages,
left:* Waxing lyrical by Anand Aithal's penthouse
pool with décor by Marlaine Collins of Tantrum
Interiors International; *right:* A wooden statue
of Krishna from Pakistan in the home of Janet
and Ron Stride. *This page:* Blushing 'rose of
Sharon' blooms in gilded coconut husks in the
Tongs' home designed by Justin Hill of Kerry
Hill Architects, Singapore. *Opposite:* Glimpses
from the homes of Sim Chen-Min, the Lees,
Genevieve and Ashley, the Strides and
Catherine LaJeunesse.

Contents

Eastern Ideals, Global Directions

"LIVING in Asia is a little bit about chaos," says architect Chan Soo Khian, challenging notions that associate serenity with the East. As lifestyles become more urban and cities more congested (Bangkok's police are delivering up to 25 babies a day in the backs of gridlocked cars, while Singaporeans have to bid for the right to even own a car), people – and their homes – are looking inward.

"Zen is here to stay," says Singapore-based interior designer Stefanie Hauger, "in the sense of a desire for a holistic lifestyle in which the home is seen as a sanctuary, with Asia having the added bonus of being surrounded by art and artefacts that stem from the very source of this new approach to living." Across the globe, from Donald Trump to Richard Branson, Prince Charles to Rob Lowe, people are using feng shui principles of placement in their homes, while the revival of the 1960s movements of minimalism and modernism can be seen as another reaction to postmodern excess. The role of the home as a tranquil refuge from the outside world has never been more important.

Just how this is being done in Asia varies. A new generation of architects (many of whom are venturing into interior design) is revealing that what is Asian extends beyond artefacts – or a lack thereof – to spatial and spiritual qualities. The way one enters a house, the hierachy of privacy, ambiguous spaces created by transitory screens and surfaces between the interior and exterior, the presence of water, the open plan, a courtyard, shadows animating a blank wall – all are a celebration of simple beauty or what the Japanese call *wabi sabi*. "It's less a recognizable look and more an attitude of how we look at space and design," says Singapore-born Yale graduate Soo Khian.

This attitude informs *New Asian Style*, whether the look is zen minimalist, contemporary ethnic, tropical modern, retro and recycled, or a fusion of two or more of these general trends, as it is most often these days. It is becoming increasingly hard to apply labels, as the examples in this book show. Thus, the pioneers of the Balinese aesthetic for residences in Southeast Asia more than a decade ago – architects like Kerry Hill and Ernesto Bedmar – are now transcending traditional archetypes in an unselfconscious contemporary tropicalism inspired in part by the work of Sri Lanka's most famous architect Geoffrey Bawa.

"We are now referencing and reinterpreting past traditions through suggestion and association rather than replication," notes Hill, whose Singapore-based company KHA designed the Datai resort in Malaysia and Amanresort's Amanusa in Bali, as well as numerous private residences for Asia's élite. His partner, Justin Hill, asserts that "decoration has had its day and we are even moving away from traditional materials". Bedmar is also experimenting with materials such as aluminium and steel as alternatives to the increasingly rare well-seasoned timber to "achieve, in a very simple way, the same poetry, homeliness and romance as traditional architecture".

While simplicity and zen 'holism' continue to be the trend (from Italian couturier Giorgio Armani's homeware collection to Singapore furniture designer Tay Hiang Liang), for most people extreme minimalism has proven too austere, impractical and downright confusing (yes, even to Asians, many of whom equate it, as one home owner says, with "an uncomfortable Italian sofa"). Regional interior designers such as Hauger and Marlaine Collins are predicting a return to comfort and an emphasis on softer interiors;

Opposite: A room with a view. Overlooking a "very Manhattan" Singapore skyline, the retro and recycled living room of an Asian-American couple's apartment features a classic art-deco sofa (Tong Mern Sern Antiques, Arts and Crafts) crafted in Singapore in the 1950s, a coffee table made from an old Indian daybed supporting Burmese lacquerware, and two Bank of China armchairs "literally picked up off the street" after they were thrown out during a renovation.

international talents such as London homeware designer and Designers Guild consultant William Yeoward are already producing luxurious fabric collections inspired by the East.

Despite the trend towards hermetically-sealed, high-rise living in space-starved urban areas in Asia – which is fostering "shiny glass boxes without a trace of soul or context", according to tropical modern architect Guz Wilkinson, there is a growing backlash against what Bali-based landscape gardener Made Wijaya calls "what passes for New Asia-*nouveau,* neo-New York or just ugly". Home owners and industry professionals such as Wijaya are taking up Indian designer Rajiv Sety's warning: "Everyone's so busy going global, they've forgotten about local!"

Whether it is the rich detail of mother-of-pearl tiles from Suluwesi or 1950s art-deco furniture crafted in Singapore, sophisticated Asians are realizing the potential of local cultural sources and design elements to impart magical moods in contemporary settings. So are their Western counterparts; David Copperfield's New York apartment conjures up a languid colonial lifestyle with poolside items such as Javanese planter's chairs; John Cougar Mellancamp sleeps in an antique Burmese teak four-poster; more contemporary Asian home accessories are being commissioned by Donna Karan, Karl Lagerfeld and Joseph from designers like Thailand's Ou Baholyodhin. Singapore-based interior designer Ed Poole, whose projects in Southeast Asia include the communist-chic House of Mao restaurants, has coined the term "urban tropic" for "the new Asian look in which modern furniture and accessories – everything from place mats to ashtrays – are being produced using indigenous materials such as coconut wood in places like Chiang Mai and Bali".

Juxtaposition is the key. Singaporean architects and interior designers Mink Tan, Sim Chen-Min and Sim Boon Yang are developing an 'ethno-modern' approach by placing focal areas of exotic details against clean, contemporary backdrops. "We want to avoid the dogmatic distinction of modern versus Asian vernacular," says Sim Chen-Min. This sentiment is echoed in the West by authorities as diverse as US-based fashion designer Vivienne Tan, whose *China Chic* takes a highly personal and provocative look at using cultural details *(cheongsams* to Qing desks) as counterpoints in Occidental settings, to UK-based interior designer Kelly Hoppen, whose East Meets West style is seen everywhere from first-class airline cabins to the homes of celebrities. As Hong Kong entrepreneur and designer of the élite China Clubs in Asia, David Tang, notes: "If you want to do a Chinese interior these days, it has to be a bit Western."

Opposite: Sharing space with the pool, the tropical modern house of Claire Chiang and K.P. Ho is supported by concrete pillars treated to resemble granite. Parts of the second floor are suspended over water, blurring boundaries and enhancing the resort feel.

Above: Bathroom bliss. In Judy and Morgan McGrath's tropical modern home, a painting by Indonesian artist Sukamto rests on an easel by the free-standing jacuzzi tub. The smoothness of the latter is a delightful contrast to the textured travertine used for the floor and shower area.

Below: Collector's corner. Antiques such as a 19th-century Burmese betelnut box (on floor at left), a 19th-century Thai *repoussé* silver bowl (on a Thai reproduction rain drum) and a Tibetan medallion rug create an exotic living space for Catherine LaJeunesse. Behind the Filipino rattan sofa (with Princess & the Pea cushions) is a Thai temple drum.

While dining under red silk lanterns and stainless-steel window bracing is not everyone's cup of *cha,* the idea of being unapologetic about the past – communist, colonial or *kampong* – is another facet of embracing what is local. Kerry Hill calls this 'authenticity': "It has to do with the genuineness of origins, a sense of belonging. It is felt as much as it is seen and evolves through intuition." However, in this age of mass communication and travel, what is local and what is universal is becoming increasingly intermixed, as Hill is the first to point out.

New Asian Style is somewhere in between local and universal, modern and ancient, chaos and calm. Nowhere in Southeast Asia is this more apparent than the former British colony of Singapore, where all the homes in this book were photographed. The vast majority of the three-million-strong population of this young city state which separated from Malaysia in 1965 lives in high-rise apartments and is comparatively well-educated (increasingly outside of Asia) and well-travelled. Moreover, as in the West, these 'New Asians' are increasingly likely to be living as single occupants or childless couples as they are in nuclear or extended families.

Such broad brushstrokes characterize the home owners and house occupants in this book who are "as distinguished by their multiplicity" as their homes, to paraphrase Singapore-based architect and author Robert Powell's definition of 'New Asian'. They are just as likely to own a second home in Bali as in London; they shop in Bandung, Bangkok and Brisbane; they tend to design at least some of their own furnishings; and some of them are not even of Asian ethnicity.

An attitude more than a given look, *New Asian Style* is above all about invention, experimentation and individuality, qualities which are unrestricted to geographic or racial boundaries. The urge to personalize one's home environment has never been so strong. As Donna Warner, editor of *Metropolitan Home,* says: "Homes are about happiness, not about being right."

Opposite: Elegant Chinese furniture such as this late Qing Dynasty blackwood reading chair characterizes this contemporary Asian interior by Stefanie Hauger and Arabella Richardson, in a shophouse renovation by Chan Soo Khian.

Tropical Modern

Opposite: Islands in the sun. The living area and a wooden pagoda appear to float on the infinity pool. Understated ornamentation outside the living area includes three roughly chiselled granite blocks and a bonsai tree.

Right: The *chenggal*-wood, oversized front door – flanked by two potted mandarin trees on the outside – confers a sense of entry.

Far right: Delaying the arrival into the central courtyard for feng shui purposes and dramatic effect, a slatted *chenggal* door affords transparency as well as privacy.

Spirit Level

Restraint as well as risk characterize the design of this refined home by Justin Hill of Kerry Hill Architects (KHA), Singapore. An exciting synergy of interior and exterior was achieved by Hill and the Tongs – two surgeons and their teenage daughter.

At the main entrance, two water gardens lap a granite walkway, creating the illusion of walking over water, a typical Asian concept. The sense of ceremony is heightened by a dense double door with a wooden bolt, reminiscent of Chinese courtyard houses, complemented by a slatted double door leading to the central courtyard. "Although this is a formal entrance the clients agreed to leave it partially open to the elements, reflecting the tropical climate as well as Singapore's slightly more casual lifestyle to that of other Asian countries," notes Hill.

A seemingly natural progression of space is one of the tenets of zen philosophy, which welcomes ambiguities between indoors and outdoors, and between public and private spaces. Such blurred divisions are underlined both in the layout and materials. The two main axes of the house provide wonderful vistas from, respectively, the living area through the courtyard to the dining room and the painstakingly tended Japanese garden; and from the much-used piano, through the living area, down the hall and the garden again. Malaysian *balau* wood, limestone and granite feature extensively inside and out, while green Chinese slate roof tiles lend a subtle Oriental nuance.

Only a few pieces of the owners' collection of traditional Chinese furniture from their previous home, a conservation shophouse in Emerald Hill, were timeless and streamlined enough to make the transition.

Much thought also went into selecting the glinting glass mosaic tiles for the pool: "We wanted a dark blue green as in Tian Hu (Heavenly Lake) in the Tian Shan mountains in Xinjiang," says the owner. Even nature conspired to create a consistently beautiful theme; algae staining the ribbed concrete pool wall a glowing copper shade which matches the timber louvres.

Opposite: The first main axis runs from the living space through the courtyard to the dining room. Dense bamboo and other tropical plants are glimpsed over and through a blind at the far end of the dining room.

Right: Levels of meaning. The view from the piano platform through the living area down the partially open hall to the Japanese-style garden. Tatami mats signal the fun and informality of the owners' piano soirées. Open on three sides, the living space features simple modern furniture in teak and natural fabrics (from The Lifeshop, Singapore and Xtra Living, Singapore) except for a few family heirlooms including a 'moonstone' marble and blackwood footstool and an altar table.

Far left: Symbolizing ripples of sand or waves, this piece in Portland stone by London-based Singaporean sculptor Kim Lim looks different depending on the light spilling into the display alcove in the living area.

Left: A few well-chosen, beautiful manmade artefacts such as this glass sculpture by Singapore's Tan Sock Fong make strong statements throughout the house.

Opposite: Table in waiting. Austere furnishings complement the dining room's strong lines and light. Asymmetrical facing walls, comprising adjustable louvres opening onto an informal sitting area on one side and a wall of cupboards on the other, add interest. Foliage from the garden and sculptural flowers such as these calla lilies adorn the dining set from Xtra Living, Singapore.

Above: Indented with a basin, an island topped with stainless steel is the centrepiece of the light, airy kitchen. Stainless steel shelving and utensils give the room an industrial feel.

Right: In the indoor-outdoor sitting/dining area adjacent to the dining room, starfruit in stunning handblown glass by Potterhaus Singapore spells simple elegance.

Opposite, clockwise from top left: Water fall: seemingly suspended in mid-air, the infinity pool challenges logical perspective in a perfect zen paradox. A clever extension of the internal stairway from the living area to the downstairs study, these external stairs hug the ridged concrete pool wall: "The owners and I spent hours sticking timber strips into the cement to achieve the desired effect," recalls Hill. Poolside, teak furniture is a delightfully sensuous contrast to concrete tiles. Leading to the downstairs study, polished limestone stairs are flanked by local *chenggal* wood and extend below the glass wall. Adjustable by hand, full-length louvres outside the main study below the living area allow quick response to climatic changes. Fully motorized articulated screens in the same wood shield at least two-thirds of the house, a study in openness in planning and contents. The infinity-edge pool disguises boundaries to give an illusion of endless space.

Right: Inspired by Japanese rock gardens *(karesansui)* but without even the embellishment of raked lines, much of the granite and gravel hardscape surrounding the house was designed by KHA, Singapore.

Opposite: Benchmark of style. Reminiscent of the open-plan lobby of a five-star tropical resort, the entertainment pavilion has lofty ceilings with exposed Indonesian teak-clad beams and full-length sliding glass doors. A rosewood bench on which Claire slept as a child (centre) and a gold and black painting of three 'eggs' representing the Hos' children by Thai artist Khun Pong Thai are highlights.

First Resort

Given their resorts' reputation as 'sanctuaries for the senses', it is not surprising that the home of Banyan Tree directors Ho Kwon Ping (K.P.) and Claire Chiang is a domestic distillation of the same principles. Like the Banyan Tree resorts in Thailand, Indonesia, the Seychelles and the Maldives, it was designed by K.P.'s brother, architect K.C. Ho, with outdoor leisure and entertaining in mind.

Excluding the separate entertainment pavilion, the pool, tennis court and house occupy roughly equal space on the extensively landscaped site. "We wanted a full-size tennis court and pool, and it was their elongated shape that dictated the design of the house," says Claire, whose busy lifestyle includes being a Singapore Member of Parliament, an author and a mother of three. "The idea was to capture as much light and air flow as possible within the best of the Asia-Pacific's tropical architectural language and complement it with an interplay of hard and soft textures. We wanted a sense of place."

The result is indeed a sanctuary for this high-profile family and their guests. The well-used tennis court has been known to fit 20 tables of ten for formal events such as fundraisers for which the couple is known. Yet despite its lofty dimensions, the space is intimate enough to honour sentimental treasures such

as a shrine to K.P.'s father, furniture from Claire's childhood and a gallery of newspaper clippings tracing K.P.'s public career – and unpretentious enough to feature a memo- and memory-laden study painted in Claire's favourite blue. Even the entertainment pavilion can be adapted to accommodate a second family if the owners' children decide to live there when adult.

The front garden is sheltered by three banyan trees imported from Malacca; one for each of the children. "With its notions of rejuvenation, strength and shelter, this magnificent exotic tree has personal as well as professional significance to us," explains Claire, who makes a point of using plants from her garden as accents throughout the house.

Above: Custom made in the US, clusters of comfortable sofas and armchairs, like this one, are interspersed with family heirlooms including Claire's 80-year-old writing table from Malacca (unseen). The entertainment pavilion is accessed directly off the entranceway, ensuring the main house remains private.

Far left: Raffles-style rattan chairs and a footstool provide attractive yet low mainten-ance poolside lounging.

Left: Welcoming gesture. A decorative iron hand made in Thailand holds flowers in a gracious grasp. "Like the English handshake, an open palm is a gesture of friend-ship in Asia – it means I have no weapon," says Claire. Available from the Banyan Tree Gallery, Singapore, the hand decoration (ideal for displaying business cards or jewellery) and heavy cotton throw, both from Thailand, rest on a colonial teakwood and wicker bench from Java.

Below left: Bold decorative statements like these hand-beaten iron candlestands on an Indonesian rice chest are points of relief along the imposing poolside walkway.

Below right: Symbolic mean-ing. At the end of a walkway between two *koi* (carp) ponds (auspicious in many Asian cultures), an elegant altar table from Malacca supports framed calligraphy represent-ing both the Hos' last name and the phrase 'Harmony is priority'. An antique gilded phoenix screen with a mirror insert, from China, symbolizes good luck and prosperity and underlines the architect's motive of delaying a full-length view of the house until the inner sanctum of the pool area is reached.

Opposite: Poolside repast. Half-glazed, cone-shaped cups on metal stands make exotic containers for flowers or refreshments. They stand on a teak and wicker tray from Thailand strewn with dried and pressed *yang* leaves. From the Banyan Tree Gallery, Singapore.

Opposite: From India and Thailand, embroidered napkins, organza bottle covers, glasses and flatware lend new life to the old marble-topped *kopitiam* table at which Claire dined as a child. The Banyan Tree Gallery, Singapore items soften the high-tech Bosch kitchen, which, like the other rooms in the house, has a view of the pool.

Above: Opening on one side to the pool and on the other to a *koi* pond shaded by melodically rustling bamboo, the minimalist dining room features a 12-seat treated teak dining table and chairs crafted in the Philippines. On the walls are two scrolls, one extolling the virtues of the banyan tree by the late Singapore calligrapher Pan Shou, and the other about the symbolism of life by a relative from Canton.

Opposite: Net gain. Draped in creamy Indian satin, the oversized four-poster in *meranti* wood is the stuff of dreams. The painting at the head of the master bed is by well-known Singaporean artist Eng Tay. The bed linen is from Banyan Tree Gallery.

Right: Chocolate-covered suite. Decorated in earth tones, the *en suite* master bathroom features Italian marble floors and walls, floor-to-ceiling teakwood louvres and mirror-image his and her vanity basins.

Below: Claire's collection of small ceramic rabbits – the Chinese zodiac animal under which she was born – nestles beneath a medicine chest.

Far Pavilions

From the moment one ventures past thick granite walls onto a wooden 'drawbridge' suspended over two ponds, poetry and romance are the order of the day. An outstanding example of contemporary tropical vernacular architecture, this two-storey home acts as a series of open-plan pavilions cooled by cross breezes from courtyards and connected by stairs and walkways.

Designed by Ernesto Bedmar, who has pioneered a kind of Balinese style for residences in Singapore, with landscaping by Bali-based Made Wijaya, the house felt so complete to owners Reeta and Sat Pal Khattar that they added only a few specially sourced furnishings. "You cannot have too many things in such an open house and we wanted to continue the feeling of simplicity," says Reeta, an artist born in Penang, Malaysia. "The colours were also important; being so close to nature we chose lots of creams to complement the greenery visible from every room."

The neutrally shaded furnishings mainly from the US are a refined, delicate counterpoint to warm tones of teak, limestone and granite. Asian accents including statues of the family's patron saint, Ganesh, a carved dancer by Balinese master N. Sugara, a cast-iron Shiva's head from southern India and a Peranakan bowl from Malacca lend context to the lofty interior.

Above: Viewed from the master bedroom pavilion, the central courtyard is dotted with palms, coral trees and frangipani. Wijaya also introduced a traditional Balinese *compang* (raised stone platform) and statuary (unseen).

Left: Now a contemporary design, the drip pattern on this water jar from Thailand (Pacific Nature Landscapes, Singapore) was derived from the days of poor glaze quality. Inspired by a hanging bird's nest, the wrought-iron outdoor lamp was designed by Made Wijaya (Pacific Nature Landscapes).

"I wanted a big benevolent Ganesh to bless and welcome everyone who enters the house," says Reeta, who shares Indian heritage with her lawyer husband. At her request, Wijaya shipped an 800 kg (120 stone), 1-m (3-ft) high *palimanan* statue of the Hindu god of auspicious beginnings from Bali and situated it at the head of the sweeping driveway fashioned from Chinese granite cobblestones.

An atmosphere of gracious living pervades whether the occasion is a breakfast for two on the verandah, complete with monogrammed English tea set, or a traditional wedding ceremony for 400, for which the house was festooned with jasmine and marigolds, with Thai-style *krathong*s (candlelit floral arrangements) floating in the ponds. "The idea behind the design was to create a tropical-style house with immense peace and security," notes Bedmar of Bedmar & Shi Designers, Singapore.

Opposite: A white cotton-wool mix sofa set from New York composed around a glass coffee table supported by two temple brackets from southern India complements the airy living room, seen here from the wooden walk-way. On the right, a camphor display cabinet containing Indian, Chinese, Balinese, Indonesian and Japanese antiques makes a rare 'busy' statement. A Kashmiri rug adds colour to the custom-made German wool carpet on the polished limestone floor.

Above: A favourite spot, the verandah features woven water-hyacinth chairs from the Philippines embracing a low table made from a glass-topped Thai pot. Other table bases in the house include a stack of books, a Chinese bamboo basket, a piece of old teak and a bullock cart.

Right: One end of the living room, from which wooden latticework doors lead to the bedroom pavilion, features a pine and marble table and leather chair from the US.

Left: Water flowing from a terracotta water storage urn from Madura makes an informal shower by the pool.

Above: The ample, grid-patterned, walk-in dressing room in *balau* wood off the master bedroom conceals clutter and underlines the house's timber theme.

Opposite: Designed to maximize light and air flow, the downstairs artist's studio – where Reeta spends much of her time – has 10-m (32-ft) high ceilings.

High Drama

With an unrivalled view of the city skyline and the indulgence of a private pool, this 10th-storey penthouse apartment demanded a distinctive decor. At the urging of New Zealand-born interior designer Marlaine Collins, tenant Anand Aithal opted for vivid jewel hues that celebrate life in the tropics.

It was a daring deviation from the neutral colours in his last two homes in Hong Kong, on which Marlaine had also worked. But it suited the strong personality and determination of the Cambridge-educated managing director at a major US investment bank. "I wanted a sanctuary from the pressures of my work," says Anand. "This apartment was perfect because it had light, high ceilings and lots of space."

Custom-made furnishings merge with minimalist and ethnic accessories including a modern mixed media painting by Chinese artist Liu Jian to create a series of striking vistas in the open-plan living area. "Nothing is too ostentatious or high-maintenance; the emphasis is on comfort and simplicity," notes Marlaine of Tantrum Interiors International, Singapore. "I like to combine the sumptuousness of fabrics, as in the curtains, with solid clean lines."

Opposite, left: "The pool has a real calming influence," notes Anand, who admits to looking at it more than swimming in it. Echoing the glittering city skyline, Balinese lanterns imbue the night-time pool terrace with magic. Poolside landscaping by Irene Lim & Associates, Singapore.

Opposite, right: High life. The view from one side of the terrace reminds Anand of night-time Hong Kong, where he lived for many years. The other side looks over Singapore's lush tropical vegetation. "The combination of rural and urban views is perfect," he says.

Left: Shades of sophistication. The enchantment of a penthouse pool lies in its proximity to more formal living areas. Multiwick candle from The Lifeshop.

Opposite: Top-level talks. Flowing around a central staircase which leads to the downstairs bedrooms and study, the open-plan living room incorporates the lounge and dining areas. Full-length sliding glass doors open directly onto a private, 12-m (40-ft) long lap pool. On the far column is a tribal shield from Borneo. 'Zen' wood and bamboo hyacinth trays and a crackled celadon vase from The Lifeshop, Singapore are Asian accents on the Italian designer coffee table. The teal armchairs in *faux* suede were custom made in Hong Kong as were the curtains in silk from Christian Fischbacher, Switzerland.

Above: Bachelor *parti*. With a custom-made futon mattress covered with a rafia and linen mix from Christian Fischbacher of Switzerland, a Balinese teak coffee table doubles as a casual daybed. In contrast are the high-backed, teak and leather formal dining chairs custom made in Hong Kong around the wenge table from B&B Italia, Singapore. The oil, *Four Dreams of You*, is by Singapore-based English artist Ann Healey.

Left: Nestled with exotic fruits in a wooden bowl, a candle from The Lifeshop, Singapore is a stunning centrepiece.

Right: Convivial colours of blue and gold signal a change in mood in the entertainment room, where an Indonesian-made wrought-iron sofa from Tequila Kola, Hong Kong, invites lounging before the television. A painting by Indian master M.F. Hussein is on the wall.

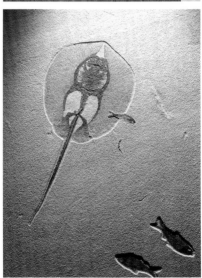

Top: Historical moment. The 160-million-year-old fossil of several nautilus shells makes a unique statement in the entrance. This fossil, and one of a stingray *(above,* a mere 55 million years old) downstairs, are from Evolution Prehistoric Art Gallery, Singapore. "I like that they are real," says Anand.

Right: Small brass figures of *nats* (Burmese mythological spirits) bought in a trinket shop in Myanmar rest on the Thai-style coffee table.

Cottage Industry

Handicraft and humour combine in this refreshingly homely house, in spite of its grand design. From whimsical wrought-iron grilles to hand-fired tiles, glittering grottos to rooftop gardens, swing seats to secret passageways, customized details evoke a sense of tradition and charm. Vernacular elements such as sloping roofs (a referral to Japanese and Chinese temples), Balinese ventilation pieces and an overall plan adapted from Asian courtyard houses place the two-storey suburban retreat firmly in its tropical context.

"The clients didn't want it to be a monster house, despite the 1,700-sq-m (18,300-sq-ft) site," recalls architect Guz Wilkinson of Guz Wilkinson Architects, Singapore. "I feel strongly that a building should be able to have ornament and decoration. We are trying to get away from the premise that less is always more, which we feel is being taken to the extreme."

The call for human-scale homes which respond to their environments has its roots in the 19th-century British Arts & Crafts Movement; little wonder that Guz cites two of that movement's leading architects as influences. One, Sir Edwin Lutyens, was known for his attention to minute details even down to the design of hand-made door locks; the other, Charles Voysey, embraced vernacular designs which integrated the garden with the interior.

Right: Balau wood was chosen for the full-length louvres between the open-air lobby and the front pond because it does not rot in wet and humid conditions. Handmade Chinese terracotta floor tiles are punctuated by decorative ceramic tiles from Italy.

Below: Carved wooden chairs from the Philippines are a handy resting point beside the thick Malaysian granite rubble wall in the entrance. The silvery quartz floor tiles are inlaid with black pebbles.

Bottom: A fine detail on a wrought-iron door by Mingly Ornamental, Singapore.

"In this house we tried to introduce private, intimate spaces, friendly and picturesque materials, and allow the owners to interact with their home," says Guz. "The space was also designed to let nature in – not through a plate glass screen but to let it grow into the house and share the spaces." Almost every room has cross ventilation and direct access to the garden. The organic approach extended to the soft landscaping by Stephen Caffyn which sought to preserve trees wherever possible while demolishing the previous house.

To the well-travelled Singaporean clients – a pilot and a banker, along with their two children – the home is the culmination of many years of thinking, dreaming and searching: "Beyond physical aesthetics, the architect has created a soulful house, open yet intimate, the inside embracing the outside, timeless yet evoking an old-world charm."

Left: Eavesdrop. A rope swing suspended from an eave outside the dining pavilion is an example of the slightly irreverent detailing for which the architect is known. Perched over a grotto glittering with gold tiles (suggesting coins), the guest pavilion opposite can also support a seat swing over the 22-m (70-ft) pool.

Above: Step in the right direction. A cast-concrete staircase capped with teak, inset with *palimanan* stone tiles from Bali (Pacific Nature Landscapes), a pre-World War II *kopitiam* table and a grass-like iron fence are highlights in the open-to-the-elements lobby. Clear glass tiles form the roof (unseen).

Opposite: Climbing up the wall. Exterior granite stair treads, cantilevered into the concrete dining-room wall, are a feature in their own right, as are the small windows which contrast with the full-length louvred ones used elsewhere throughout the house. The lazy susan supports a trio of camellias arranged on Potterhaus glassware by Cecilia Ng Lay Kuan of Woodsville Florist, Singapore whose clients include The Ritz-Carlton Millenia Singapore. The Russian Empire dining table and chairs are from Giemme Stile's Classical Collections.

Right: Luxuriously textured fabrics such as this hand-embroidered velvet throw and hand-painted velvet cushion covers from India and pleated silk on the Jim Thompson footstools personalize the formal lounge area. Throw and cushions are from Mara Miri, Singapore.

Opposite: Bathing beauty. Malaysian *pom-poms,* similar to chrysanthemums (Far East Oriental), lend natural luxury to the master bath enthroned on a platform of honed black granite. The indoor-outdoor feel is accentuated by the full-length *balau* wood louvres, plants and natural elements including a stunning mounted nautilus shell with silver detailing from Bali (Pagoda House Gallery) and a *nito* basket from the Philippines (Jim Thompson). Silk bath-robe from Jim Thompson.

Left: As delightful as its cottage-like exterior, the interior of the guest pavilion features an antique Italian wrought-iron four poster. Its filigree work is comple-mented by an intricately hand-embroidered quilt and pillow covers, and cushion covers with crystal detailing, all from India (Club 21 Gallery, Singapore). Old Chinese ginger jars with 'double-happiness' motifs form the bedside lamp bases.

Above: Wet and wild. Orchids, greenery and sunlight are constant companions in the guest pavilion bathroom, thanks to *balau* shutters and cut-outs. Quartz tiles inlaid with black pebbles cover the floor and lower part of the wall, the top of which is finished with black granite. On the pebble window-sill is a Thai wrought-iron candle-stand with mouth-blown glass shield (Jim Thompson).

Global Warming

Satay and silver; biscotti and batik. Designed by the late American modern architect Paul Rudolph, this magnificent mansion's grand proportions complement its expatriate tenants' extensive collection of Asian artefacts. Yet idiosyncratic touches of whimsy, a street-smart sense of innovation and attention to homely details add unexpected character to this family home where as much care is taken hosting a children's scout meeting as a dinner for the board of directors.

The entrance to the vast downstairs vestibule is surveyed by two life-sized Thai temple disciples in bronze. These, in turn, flank an equally imposing lacquered Burmese Buddha. Pieces of such stature would crowd more conventional homes but sit beautifully in these lofty, light-filled spaces where different floor levels and partitions create a multitude of vistas. Indeed, they are often displayed symmetrically to achieve a sense of order and intimacy, as in the glass-sided living room where a 14th-century Ganesh from central Java balances a composition of three *mataban* burial jars from Vietnam and Borneo and two *lamaris* (cabinets) framing a 12th-century stone Buddha.

The unapologetically public-building atmosphere is further softened by Laotian and Thai temple flags strung between pillars, Persian and Pakistani carpets, and rare *ikats*, batiks, silks and other textiles used as runners on cabinets, altar tables and wedding chests. On these nestle eclectic pan-Asian items such as *ani-ani* (ceremonial rice cutters), *hsun-oks* (offering containers), betelnut boxes, porcelain pillows and silver pumpkins. A piece of glass carried by two Chinese ceramic elephants, the living-room coffee table bears treasures ranging from Cambodian weaving utensils to hornbill-bird bone earrings carved by the Dayaks of Kalimantan. Near the billiard table, a Javanese *wayang kulit* puppet proffers the eight ball on its oil-lamp tray.

"People say it looks like a museum but feels like a home," says Californian Judy McGrath of the house she shares with her investment banker husband Morgan and their children.

Above: Not for the vertically challenged, a Straits Chinese wedding bed in the master bedroom features a batik bedspread by Asmoro of Jakarta. The scroll tray is from the Four Seasons Resort Sayan, Bali.

Right: Blue and white china trade pieces purchased during the McGraths' last posting in Jakarta grace a *huanghuali* chest laden with chopstick rests from Cambodia, napkin rings from Bangkok and English cutlery. Delicate latticework on two tapered *huanghuali* cabinets containing family heirlooms (unseen) also contribute to the room's airy feel.

Left: Hand-carried from Hanoi, a protective *bodhisattva* in gold leaf and lacquer in the dining room is an attractive alternative to the ubiquitous Buddha figure.

Below left: The sinuous forms of these *huanghuali* dining chairs (House of Huanghuali, Singapore) are in sympathy with tropical tendrils outside.

Below right: An antique *obi* table runner and fusion-food tableware (The Link Home) dress the 12-seat dining table formed from a custom-made, 3-m (10-ft) long sheet of glass atop twin Ming-style *huanghuali* side tables. Huanghuali benches each sit two guests at either end.

Left, clockwise from top left: Satay is served in Balinese ceramics in celadon shades; sticky rice in pandan leaves; Judy's fine English cutlery; coconut-wood utensils and crockery stored in the rare, wheeled Indonesian *lamari* (cabinet) in the kitchen.

Opposite: Jelly beans in a Balinese ceramic dish depicting Dewi Sri, the goddess of rice and fertility (foreground), add a touch of domesticity to the industrial-style kitchen. A 19th-century Dutch colonial water filter from Yogjakarta occupies a corner on the back shelf. Gourmet Judy, who has Italian ancestry, conducts cooking classes at the restaurant-standard hob designed for hot Asian cooking. School homework and informal meals are completed on the round, marble-topped, *kopitiam* table by the full-length glass window which, like the skylight, provides a constant reminder of the equatorial surroundings. As in the rest of the house, colours are restricted so as not to clash with the vibrant outside view.

Contemporary Ethnic

Opposite: From pillar to post. A polished black granite lap pool framed by solid teak columns bisects the open-plan ground floor, defining living and dining areas which mirror each other in arrangement and design. A slatted *chenggal* skylight and the open back door (from a Chinese courtyard house) provide the only natural light.

Right: Wall candles add an almost Gothic touch.

Double Vision

In keeping with the traditionally insular form of Singapore's prewar shophouses, this Architectural Heritage Award-winning property is a tranquil urban retreat. However, where most of these late 19th-century row houses were typically long and narrow (20–40 m long and 5 m wide [66–130 ft x 16 ft]), SCDA architect Chan Soo Khian doubled the space by combining two adjacent sites. The result is an exciting open-plan interpretation in which the symmetry of architecture suggested a symmetry of interior design.

"Although difficult and challenging due to the central collonade, the architectural space almost whispered its secrets into our ears," recalls Stefanie Hauger (now with Vanilla Design), who worked with fellow interior designer Arabella Richardson. Their client, a young American accountant, had requested an elegant, stylish, "different" home where she could entertain professionally and personally, as well as "hang out " after a hard day's work. The brief perfectly matched the feeling of sanctuary evoked by the shophouse structure and the designers' reputation for introducing rugged, raw or retro elements – sculptures, fabrics, artificial flowers and plants, carvings and antique furniture – into polished modern interiors.

Formal urban Chinese furniture, including reproduction Ming Dynasty chairs and an altar table, are textural and cultural counterpoints to two large reproductions of 12th-century Khmer sculptures in cement.

Rough jute, palatial silks and tailored striae cotton in restrained shades of mint and earth tones complement the dominant downstairs architectural statements made by the central lap pool and timber columns. Upstairs, a buttery yellow is the backdrop to striking wrought-iron features in the master bedroom and is continued in the *en suite* bathroom and dressing room.

Highly convincing yet low in maintenance, artificial arrangements such as a Phalaenopsis orchid plant on the custom made, wrought-iron and glass coffee table and slip-on, striae cotton dining chair covers suit the tenant's busy lifestyle. Quirky interest relieves the structured atmosphere: poolside cushions invite leisurely lounging; wooden Indian wall brackets carved like haughty birds bear candles; bamboo birdcages bought for a song draw the eye upwards from the dining area to the second-floor landing; a series of lacquered head rests from China and Vietnam on the ledge of the upstairs walkway beg further inspection.

"An important idea in conserved shophouses is that of 'procession', where movements are choreographed to the architecture's rhythm and spaces," says Chan. Thus, the kitchen – the main portal to the frenetic outer world – is the least vernacular room while the former central air-well where the family would once gather remains the heart of the house.

Above: Chik-chak and chit-chat. Two silver geckos – onomatopoeically nicknamed *chik-chaks* in Southeast Asia after their melodic cries – are a whimsical addition to the table. Their real-life counterparts are also in residence. From John Erdos Gallery, Singapore.

Right: Requiring little light, these onion plants are suitably sculptural.

Far right: Nesting instinct. Smooth limestone eggs in a chiselled 'nest' from Java are a tactile and visual delight.

Left: A custom-made silk table runner and an artificial arrangement of artichoke hearts and blade grass (Studio 78, Singapore) pick up the mint green controlling colour downstairs. Exquisite Murano glass-beaded shades (from Heal's in London) illuminate each place setting. Two-toned Pierre Frey striae-cotton slip-covered dining chairs dress up the teak dining table. A long vertical wooden banner with a gilded 'good luck' message in Chinese characters, once mounted outside a house or shop, emphasizes the height of the room, as does the exotic *Raphis exelsa* palm (Pacific Nature Landscapes) in the niche next to it.

Opposite, clockwise from top left: Wrought-iron chairs on the exterior patio are silhouetted behind bamboo chicks; rattan *takraw* balls – used for playing a kind of volleyball with the feet in Thailand – are a rustic focal point on the formally upholstered footstool; stems of 'lucky bamboo' – displayed during Chinese New Year – spiral sensuously from a simple glass vase and last for months; their dried counterparts impart perennial style; horsehair calligraphy brushes with lacquered handles; ceramic mandarins are an unusual juxtaposition against a German wine poster.

Right: Rest and repose. A late Qing Dynasty blackwood reading chair is draped with a customized Jim Thompson silk throw with cotton *ikat* border. An original glass ship's buoy balances delicately on a fine blackwood side table. Reflected in the Republican-era Chinese mirror on the wall (which would have contained a piece of Dali marble, embroidery or semi-precious stone relief) are glass medicinal bottles (Tong Mern Sern Antiques, Arts and Crafts) and a reproduction of a late 12th-century head of Khmer King Jayavarman VII in Bayon style. The latter rests on a reproduction Ming Dynasty altar table in old chicken-wing wood.

Opposite: Fabric remnants woven through the rungs of wooden Chinese peasant ladders from China make a captivating wall feature in the master bedroom.

Right: Yellow sets off the strong lines of the master bed, lamp bases and Indian art piece – all in wrought iron. The rich quilted piqué cotton bedspread and matching curtains and lampshades in smoky grey and buttercup Houles fabric were custom designed. Single stems of orchids in white celadon vases echo the main colour.

Below left: A lacquered praying monk from Myanmar, gilded baroque mirror and crackled white celadon soap bowl from Thailand are Asian accents in the bright yellow master bathroom. Celadon bowl, soap 'eggs' and bath oils from Club 21 Gallery, Singapore.

Below right: Cast in stone. Votive candles in a stone tray (Club 21 Gallery) adorned with orchids rest on the beige terrazzo floor.

Colourful Character

Vibrant and earthy, the décor of this semi-detached colonial home reflects its tenants' colourful backgrounds and personalities. Filipino Isabel Mendezona met her Korean–Filipino husband-to-be Ron Ramos, while studying in the US. They have since lived in Hong Kong, Japan, Korea and now Singapore, where they rent a government-owned 'black and white', a former British army officer's house.

"Red and yellow make me happy; they remind me of my childhood in Cebu and have something to do with my Spanish blood," says Isabel, sipping sangria at a friend's 40th birthday party. "Green is cooling. A strictly black and white house would be depressing."

The party is one of many hosted in the courtyard, the dominant wall of which is lime green, which complements the mustard tones on a smaller wall and walkway. A homemade bamboo screen shades the table while an ice-filled, polka-dotted bathtub, on wheels, does duty as a drink station. Big, bright candles on Chinese ceramic stools and in *capiz* shell holders from the Philippines are decorative even unlit. A massive, mossy cement bas-relief of Ganesh from Yogjakarta, Indonesia, prompts conversation, as does the use of old Filipino charcoal-heated irons as ashtrays. The ever-present trickle of water from a simple bamboo pipe fixed to a Balinese urn – one of Ron's weekend projects – is a soothing counterpoint.

The riot of rich colour continues in the more formal living- and dining rooms, where paintings by Vietnamese artists such as Le Thuy vie for attention with old wooden wall panels, antique chests and chairs, lacquered pieces, baskets and soft furnishings from all over Asia. With two children, two cats and three dogs, however, the home is practical as well as stylish. An example of this is how the children have their own Thai *khantokes* (tray tables) for snacks.

A self-confessed 'frustrated interior designer', Isabel began importing homewares after friends kept on asking her how she assembled her medley of ethnic accents. "I don't follow a particular style," she muses. "I follow my heart and what moves me personally, and sometimes I go through many variations before I am satisfied. I'm not afraid of experimenting."

Above: Wooden Japanese candlesticks complement wall panels from Chiang Mai, Thailand.

Opposite, clockwise from top left: "I like the shapes," says Isabel of her collection of cast-iron Japanese teapots, one of which is shown here; a gift from an old Japanese friend in her 70s, these wooden slippers were worn by her when she was in her early teens; a bamboo umbrella stand in the entrance supports paper parasols originally carried by monks in Myanmar; a bamboo water feature in the courtyard; a tassel assembled by Ron from a shell collected by Isabel's father; mother-of-pearl shell tassels, hand-carved in the Philippines, are among ethnic accents that Isabel imports for friends and clients.

Right: Four timber temple panels – bought along a country road in Korea – are the backdrop for a gold lacquered plate from Vietnam, an old red lacquered plate from Myanmar and a fruit bowl laminated with a type of seed from the Philippines. They rest on a Korean chest.

Right: "We live out here," Isabel says about the central courtyard, where black and white architectural features are softened with colourful ethnic accents including a flock of carved wooden garudas (the consort of Vishnu in the *Ramayana*) flying across the mustard-coloured walkway wall (unseen), candles and plenty of foliage. When not employed washing dogs or children, a cast-iron bath, salvaged from the original house, serves as an over-sized ice bucket brimming with Tsingtao beer and champagne.

Left: Party girl. Accompanied by sangria and champagne, Spanish omelette and olives, paella and parmesan, tortilla and chorizo sausage, tempt the senses on a traditional northern Thai *khantoke* (tray table). A twig table runner from the Philippines, a table-cloth from Provence and ladles from South Africa complement the eclectic fare.

Below: Woven from palm leaves in the southern Philippines, this cushion cover complements a rattan magazine basket, also from the Philippines, in the upstairs master bedroom.

Right: Pure cotton, hand-embroidered bedlinen from Hanoi, Vietnam makes an elegant statement in the unfussy master bedroom. A Chinese wedding cabinet, unusually featuring square brassware instead of the traditional round, is a stunning storage device. The rattan lamp shades for the wall-mounted reading lights are from IKEA.

Above: A nod to the house's colonial past, reproductions of old Dutch planter's chairs on the porch are dressed with cushions covered with Indonesian cotton in an *ikat* design. Complementing the dominant architectural colours, the inexpensive black and white Balinese parasols were purchased in a local market near Ubud, Bali.

Right: A natural alternative to glass or plastic, these light shades crafted in the Philippines from *capiz* shell, look good by day or night.

Opposite: Mystery and majesty. Buried in central Java for hundreds of years, this andesite stone Buddha imparts a sense of gravity to the living area. Seated on a double-lotus throne with a flame as a backslab, it is attended by female deities, also in volcanic andesite and once part of a temple wall, terracotta piggy-banks and a Avoloketisvara god figure, all from the Java region and dating between the 8th and 14th centuries. On the floor is a Kirmar rug from Phalavi, Southern Iran.

Figuratively Speaking

Not everyone has the sense of drama to live with a 1.25-m (4-ft) 10th-century stone Buddha in their entrance or lifelike effigies from a Torajan tomb outside their bedroom. "A friend once said that she felt hundreds of eyes upon her when she entered," laughs Janet Stride of her tendency to collect figurative pieces and paintings. From Chicago and New York respectively, Janet and her management consultant husband Ron have lived in Southeast Asia for 25 years, including 14 in their city apartment in Singapore.

Most of the Strides' pieces are also distinctive because of Janet's personal approach to collecting. Leading museum study groups and tours in Singapore and Jakarta, Indonesia, she knows intimately the story behind each one – whether it is an intricately carved silver betelnut set from Sumatra or an oil by Nyoman Gunarsa, Indonesia's outstanding painter, whom she has known for 15 years.

From art, carpets, ceramics, jewellery, beaded artefacts, betelnut-chewing equipment, *kris* (swords),

snuff bottles, Han Dynasty soldiers and puppets to probably their most important collections of Indonesian textiles, stone and terracotta, many of the Strides' pieces are museum-standard not only for their quality but for their painstakingly researched history and careful display. Custom-made Perspex stands, tables and cabinets and perfectly placed glass shelves – all professionally lit – set off the most intricate and unusual items and ensure there is always space for one more object.

Probably their most talked about figures are a pair of early 20th-century tomb statues (*tau taus*) from Toraja in Sulawesi, Indonesia, acquired more than 15 years ago. "The practice of the *tau taus* developed from animism and the belief that the figures would carry the spirit of the deceased," Janet says. "I have seen a modern funeral where the wooden figure is still present but there is a Christian minister presiding over the ceremony. Some people might find them spooky but we see them as protectors of the house."

Above: In the living room, a Thai coffee table and side tables custom made for display contain opium weights from Myanmar; gold and silver wedding jewellery from Sumatra; silver bracelets from Timor; and a gold comb from Padang, West Sumatra, all antique. On the walls hang paintings by Balinese artists Nyoman Gunarsa (left) and Surita (right), the frames of which were also created by the painters. To the left of the Nyoman painting sits an antique black stone Buddha from India; to the right, an antique four-armed Vishnu from central Java. The red and gold sofa is by Carl Ettensperger of Wimberly, Allison, Tong & Goo.

Left: Shelf life. Pottery from China including a lovely Tang Dynasty-era dancer displaying Persian influences (top shelf) indicates the presence of foreigners in China as early as 600AD. Two rare painted pottery equestrians also from the Tang Dynasty (c. 700AD, second shelf from the top), an extremely rare bronze elephant and rider from the Majapahit period of East Java (14th century, third shelf from top), Neolithic pottery jars from Gansa, China (third shelf from top) and a Song Dynasty celadon bowl from China (9th–11th century) found in Indonesia (bottom shelf) are other highlights. To the right kneel early 20th-century figures of the Rice Goddess Dewi Sri and her Consort from central Java or Bali.

Opposite (clockwise from top left): Unfired clay pieces dating from the 14th century, with Majapahit hairstyles (one shown); this 19th-century blackwood voodoo charm of the Batak tribe from Sumatra has human hair; two Mongolian snuff bottles, made of agate with coral stoppers, stand before a rare painted terracotta statue of a man riding on a horse (c. 700AD); made of silver and gold to indicate the wealth of their owners, these portable betelnut sets from Sumatra were part of the regalia for royalty in Southeast Asia until the 20th century; displayed on a custom-made Perspex stand, this beaded ceremonial jacket was worn by a chieftain's wife in Kalimantan in the 19th and early 20th centuries; a rare Mongolian violin given to the Dalai Llama's entourage during his first visit to Mongolia in 1997.

Right: Depicting Southeast Asian scenes, art by Balinese (Dewi Nyoman Jati and Nyoman Gunarsa), Vietnamese (P.T. Laut and Pham Viet Hong Lam), Colombian (Lewis Physioc) and British (George Graham) painters punctuate the dining-room walls. Defining the entrance to the room are 19th-century *wayang golek* puppets from Central Java representing figures from the Indian epic, the *Ramayana.* Resting on the antique Japanese *obi* table runner are two terracotta piggy-banks in the style of the 14th-century Majapahit era of eastern Java. The Persian rug is from Isfahan.

Opposite: "I like walls with a lot of things on them," says Janet of her painting collection, among which is one of three women by well-known Balinese artist Kriyono (back wall). The largest painting on the left is *Thousand-hand Buddha* by Singapore-based David Kwo. To the right of this is a lacquer painting by Hoa Sy Cong Quog Ha from Hanoi, Vietnam.

Left: Carved to represent the deceased, these statues *(tau taus)* guarded a tomb in Toraja (part of which is now Sulawesi, Indonesia). Reputedly the world's most difficult cloth to make, the double *ikat* draping them is woven only in three places: India, Bali and Japan. The cloth worn by the woman figure was made in India in the 19th century yet arrived in Toraja through trade.

Below: A custom-made Perspex stand was ordered for this 19th-century gilded silver bride's headpiece from Minangkabau, Sumatra.

Opposite: Made of silver and gold, these portable betelnut sets from Sumatra have floral designs reflecting regional variations. Although not nearly as widespread since the advent of manufactured cigarettes, the social tradition of chewing a betel quid continues in Southeast Asia.

Right: Modern *losel* dolls, handmade by Tibetan monks who live with the Dalai Llama at Dharamsala, India are an interesting juxtaposition to the 19th-century Javanese *wayang kulit* puppets placed nearby. Janet imports the dolls, each one of which takes 10 monks up to a month to make, to raise funds for Tibetan refugees.

Below left: A 16th-century silver *kris* (sword) from Java on the sitting-room coffee table. "Warriors would put their *kris* under their pillow on the eve of battle and if there was blood on the blade in the morning, they believed they would win," says Janet.

Below right: Preferred by inland peoples of Borneo over gold as a sign of wealth, these beaded artefacts include a baby carrier with symbols warding off evil spirits, a covered box and a ceremonial belt.

Home Grown

A sensitive reinterpretation of local history, this renovated prewar bungalow was the childhood home of former Singapore president, Ong Teng Cheong, in the late 1940s. Owner Stanley Tan, who is Mr Ong's nephew, enlisted architect and interior designer Sim Boon Yang of eco-id, Singapore, to create a more contemporary environment without losing the old charm. "I wanted a contemporary classic style because the architecture is classical and yet Peranakan colonial," says the founder and partner of Immortal Design, a graphic design company, and director of the family's Link group of designer homeware and clothing stores.

Built in 1913, the original two-bedroom house was raised on concrete stilts to attract breezes and deter cobras and tigers. Reflecting the baroque Chinese and Malay influences common to houses built by the middle and upper classes in Southeast Asian countries under British colonial rule, it had embellished cornices and columns inset with colourful tiles featuring auspicious floral and animal motifs. Phoenixes (representing female energy), dragons (male energy) and lions and bird of paradise blooms are depicted against cobalt-blue and flamingo-pink backgrounds. These were protected during the renovation, although the original ornate staircase was replaced with 10 simple cement slabs on steel, achieving a sleeker, more modern feel.

The main house was partitioned into living (including drawing, reception and family rooms) and dining sections, guest and family bedrooms with a separate outhouse for the kitchen, bathroom and servants. The renovation substituted timber columns with concrete beams, removed walls to create a more open living area, added luminous, spa-like bathrooms to the main house by expanding it into the backyard and replaced the old garage with a stunning dining-kitchen pavilion. While full-length glass windows on three sides and a 5-m (16-ft) high ceiling give the new structure an al fresco feel, its external pillars have the same recessed line detailing and motifs as the main house.

Right: Shaded by a frangipani tree, an open-air courtyard between the main house and the dining-kitchen pavilion is a great place for a picnic. This view of the Indonesian colonial-style chair and table is from the enclosed walkway connecting the main house with the new pavilion. The cement slabs used outside are complemented by aged sile stone on the floor of the dining pavilion and bathrooms, chosen for its cooling quality and neutral colour.

The interior is sophisticated and muted, thanks to discreet lighting, natural materials including the original teak floors and sandblasted sile (reconstituted) stone, and old and new furnishings chosen for their simple, elegant lines. These include inherited pieces, mostly from Stanley's grandparents on both sides (including his paternal grandfather, rubber king and founder of Nanyang University, Tan Lark Sye, who was the ex-president's father), which represent colonial art-deco style during the modernization period of Southeast Asia from 1920 to the '50s.

Reviving the *kampong* atmosphere of bygone days, the garden is dense with heliconia, traveller's and sago palms, fruit trees such as *jambu*, starfruit, banana and tamarind, and vegetables including sweet potato and pink-flowered torch ginger, all of which Stanley plants and tends himself – a rarity in this space-starved city. "The house used to face a banana plantation and overlooked the old Kallang airport runway and it still has chickens running around it and street peddlers out the front," he says. "That's what I love most; its history and character."

Above: Flight of fantasy. A detail of the original Peranakan tiles, depicting a phoenix and flowers.

Far left: Used in the house's original garden, this stone and cement stool is an example of typical prewar tropical garden furniture. Elsewhere in the garden are old dragon pots from China and a traditional Malay coconut-leaf broom *(sapu lidi),* recalling the handicrafts of yesteryear.

Left: Bought by Stanley's father in Taiwan in the 1970s, this granite lion is one of a pair mounted in the pond, which acts as a threshold tying together the main house and the dining pavilion. The entrances of many Asian buildings have representations of a lion (with a ball) and a lioness (with a cup) to attract prosperity.

Opposite: Muted appeal. The lounge features Stanley's grandparents' art-deco teak armchairs, and modern Italian black leather sofas, originally his sister's, set off by Thai silk cushions in earthy tones (Link Home). Three Vietnamese lacquered bowls and a Thai bronze Buddha sit on the steel and walnut-stained coffee table designed by Stanley. The lamps are by French interior designer Christian Liaigre; flowers by Sebastian for The Link. A Pakistani rug rests on the old teakwood floor.

Right: In the dining-kitchen pavilion, the trusses were left exposed for texture and to accentuate the ceiling height. An arrangement of tamarind twigs from the garden, flanked by two Vietnamese black lacquered vases (Link Home) on the art-deco sideboard, looks like sketched lines on a canvas against the 'floating wall' separating dining and food-preparation areas (background). To the left is a painting by the Singaporean artist Paul Tan. Stanley's grandparents' 1940s art-deco teak breakfast table and chairs anchor the light-filled dining area, which has full-length glass doors on three sides. Handmade fans from Stanley's collection spanning China, Korea, Thailand and Indonesia mark each fusion-food setting (Link Home), while freshly picked sweet potato and bougainvillaea vines crown a Christian Tortu resin vase (Link Home).

Opposite: Low-slung modern Thai teak furniture (Sensual Living, with cushion from Princess & The Pea) is both practical and elegant, as is the non-slip granolithic finish in the central courtyard.

Right: While much of the original exterior, including the knuckle-shaped windows (top right) and pendant lamp, has been retained, the traditional pastel shades have been replaced by cream with grey accents. An Indonesian mat, made of wooden tiles knitted together with wire, lies on the cement floor, which was covered with ornate tiles.

Shop Talk

This breathtakingly modern translation of turn-of-the-century shophouse architecture is as intelligent and global as its tenants. Half-Japanese, half-American anthropologist Elizabeth MacLachlan and her British husband David Skillen have decorated the prewar terrace house in sympathy with its mixed cultural heritage. Just as its façade is an elaborate medley of Chinese, Malay, European and colonial elements, so their collectibles range from Japanese and Chinese sake cups through primitive textiles from Bali and Laos to Singapore art-deco dining- and armchairs.

Far from overwhelming the rigorously minimal design achieved by the shophouse's owner and interior designer/architect Sim Boon Yang, the items displayed have been tightly edited. "I hate clutter," attests Elizabeth in a philosophy shared by eco.id senior partner Boon. Cement floors and steel finishes are softened by natural elements such as a grove of mature tree ferns and frangipani, slate walls and timber decking, textiles and terracotta pots, and bold arrangements of red ginger and bamboo.

The spartan, industrial-feel foyer is tempered by a magnificent composition of two Chinese temple doors – sold by Balestier Road junk shop dealer Jerry Kwan on the condition that should the couple ever leave Singapore, they would sell the doors back to him at the original price – and a pair of antique Ming-style horseshoe chairs.

In the master bathroom, a chunky laundry sink, picked up from a demolition waste skip, is juxtaposed with sleek modern fittings. "Its simple, block-like proportions are compatible with the attempt to keep the design subtly modern yet seamless with the shophouse atmosphere," notes Boon.

The central courtyard, where a 5-m (16-ft) pool has usurped the former *koi* pond, continues to command importance. "The indoor-outdoor lifestyle and the community feeling is unique," says Elizabeth.

Left: Linked by the colour blue on the wall opposite the sofa set in the downstairs lounge are, *clockwise from top left*, a collection of sake and tea cups from China and Japan (including Elizabeth's grandfather's favourite cup); a Taisho-era (1863–1923) Japanese farmer's jacket made from paper and indigo cloth; a turquoise-glazed, tea-drying container from China (Eastern Discoveries Antiques, Singapore); and a Balinese wedding chest supporting old water jugs from Luang Prabang, Laos.

Opposite, clockwise from top left: Stained with a century's worth of incense oil, these Chinese temple doors are a wall feature in the foyer; a pair of tatami and velvet *geta,* men's traditional Japanese slippers, rests on the front door mat; a 1930s standing fan (C.K. Collections) made in the US occupies a corner of the downstairs lounge area; 2,000-year-old Han Dynasty terracotta figures on a ledge in the dining area; in the upstairs lounge, two puppet masks from Zimbabwe are points of interest on a side table; well-worn, brass tattoo implements from Pagan, Myanmar march across a coffee table formed by pushing two large wicker baskets together in the downstairs lounge. On a nearby wall (unseen) hangs a framed muslin cloth, covered with tattoo designs, bought in a curio shop near Inle Lake, Myanmar. It is stained with sweat and blood where it was placed on skin when a design was traced.

Right: An Akha hill-tribe woman's costume, bought in the used-clothing section of Chiang Mai's night market, Thailand and an antique Balinese *ikat,* a wedding gift from an antique dealer friend, are displayed on the main wall in the downstairs lounge. A metal rice bowl from Luang Prabang, Laos, and a porcupine-quill hat from South Africa sit on side tables. A blue *kilim* adds colour to the cement floor. "We have mostly *kilims* because they feel cooler than Persian rugs and we prefer their colourful abstract geometrical designs over the subtle and intricate patterns of the Persian rugs," says Elizabeth. Thai silk cushions from Princess & The Pea complement the elegant grey base cushions of the custom-made rattan sofa set (Hor Cane Furniture, Singapore). Unlike in traditional shophouses, which tend to be dark, Boon has incorporated light into the succession of spaces which remain faithful to the original architecture, as in this room.

Above left: "Far from the madding crowd". "The shop-house is in one of the busiest areas, yet is green and spacious," says Elizabeth. The poolside slate feature wall is repeated in the lounge and outdoor bathroom.

Left: Surgical precision. Crowned by an operating theatre lamp from the former Singapore Children's Hospital, the table is set for another night of cross-cultural conversation. To the right is an old Balinese *ikat*.

Above: A table runner from Luang Prabang, Laos accentuates the 3.6-m (12-ft) length of the dining table, set with Elizabeth's grandfather's 1922 wedding china and encircled by non-matching 1950s British colonial art-deco chairs (Tong Mern Sern Antiques, Arts and Crafts, David's Antiques and Roger's Carved Furniture). Across the courtyard is a loose ikebana arrangement of six bamboo poles, beyond which is a lounge separated from the foyer by a *nyatoh* half wall.

Opposite: In the study, a Sumatran textile displaying two types of *ikat* weaving, complements the salmon tones of the bed linen from Princess & The Pea. Other textiles from Bali, Laos and Japan rest on the rungs of a bamboo ladder.

Right: On a 19th-century red datewood scroll table, a 19th-century Chinese saddle ornament is flanked by the remains of old 8th-century pottery jars salvaged from an archaeological dig in Pagan, Myanmar. "We rescued them from a garbage heap which workers were hauling into a cement mixer, to make bricks," recalls Elizabeth. To the left of the table on the floor are Chinese army boots, made of leather with iron cleats underneath, a first wedding anniversary gift for Elizabeth from David. To the right is the centre-piece of a gristmill from Indonesia, refashioned as a vase with legs. Underneath rests a xylophone from Myanmar. On the wall is a woodblock print of a folk figure entitled *Crazy Oschichi Climbing a Fire Tower* (1985) by the late Japanese artist Yoshitoshi Mori.

Below left: A ceramic sake jar in the upstairs sitting room.

Below right: A bamboo tray holds lacquered horsehair tea-cups and a chainmail-draped water jug from India on the coffee table of the upstairs lounge.

Zen Minimalist

Previous page, main picture: Altared state. An abstract oil painting by Ashley in the palest of pinks appears mounted on a stainless-steel table constructed as a one-off for an advertising shoot.

Right: The graceful curve of a standing Arco lamp – Castiglioni's 1962 answer to the problem of stylishly lighting a dining table – contributes to the zen mood of the dining area. A Florence Knoll marble-topped oval dining table with a chrome base (instead of plastic as in the original Saarinen design) is accompanied by Mies Van der Rohe office-style chairs in alacantara and chrome.

Breathing Space

From Christie's to crystals, this marble and metal minimalist apartment reflects its owners' appreciation for the material and the metaphysical – and their cross-cultural roots. Singapore-born Genevieve runs an advertising agency as well as a holistic spa called Breathing Space while Australian partner Ashley represents 'street furniture' manufacturer J.C. Decaux in Asia. After Sim Boon Yang of eco.id worked on their offices, the couple asked him to transform their inner-city apartment into "a respite from this urban landscape; a serene space to go after a difficult day".

Two limited-edition HK97 chairs by hot Anglo-Thai designer Ou Baholyodhin are pieces of art in their own right in the buffed marble entranceway which spills into the open-plan living-dining area. There, classics such as US designer Ludwig Mies Van der Rohe's 1930s leather and steel daybed, Italian Achille Castiglioni's 1962 Arco dining-table lamp and a Florence Knoll version of US architect Eero Saarinen's 1950s marble dining table continue the impact. While such pieces can hardly be described as humble, their spare design fits well into the owners' minimalist mission to banish clutter and excess.

A zen approach is further underlined by sliding doors and partitions, the use of alcoves (including one in the corridor to the bedrooms harbouring a small but

Above: Another design classic, this 1930s daybed by Mies Van der Rohe upholstered in black leather is positioned to divide the dining area from the lounge space in the open-plan living room which is flooded with light on two sides.

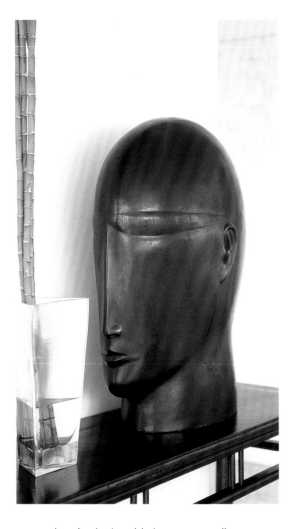

Far left: An imposing granite and concrete sculpture by South African Anton Schmidt adds a human element to the deliberately clinical living area. A glass vase containing five stems of lucky bamboo on the Ming-style elm altar table and a cowhide are other organic influences.

Left: Asian clients including Abode in Tokyo and Jim Thompson in Bangkok were quick to embrace Ou Baholyodhin's minimalist creations which followed this award-winning HK97 chair, of which only 97 were made to mark Hong Kong's handover to China; the rest of the world began to sit up and listen after fashion icons Karl Lagerfeld, Kenzo, Joseph, Donna Karan and Madonna started working with him.

Opposite: Less is more in the living-dining area which is "devoid of excess", according to architect/interior designer Sim Boon Yang – a result of working within an existing space and a limited budget.

comprehensive bar) and ledges, an overall openness and emphasis on natural light, and a profound sense of 'asymmetrical' balance in the arrangement of objects and furniture. The combined living space gives the occupants room to breathe and contemplate textures and tones. The only thing that could be remotely accused of looking – at least a little – cluttered are the books on three wall-to-wall, custom-made shelves in the study. Their unconcealed spines offer an insight into their owners' diverse interests which include health, personal development, style, Asian culture and maps.

Feminine touches such as candles flickering on a black lacquered Burmese offering tray supported by a concrete-plastered plinth outside the front door, three crystal balls sifting sunlight on a window ledge, a textured pale pink abstract oil painting by Ashley

(precisely spotlighted from above), crystal jewellery 'energizing' in a glass and mirror pyramid crafted by a Bali-based French artisan and family photographs slotted into Perspex frames in the bedroom are the yin to the apartment's colder yang elements. So are subtly luxurious elements such as white linen napkins and good black coffee; double curtains for Sunday sleep-ins; and crisp cotton slipcovers on a comfortable bed-room armchair, upon which rests a black leather bear.

Subscribing to the view that "discipline is libera-tion", Genevieve refuses to bring home the cross-cultural residential sculptures she is designing under the Mandarin Orange label for fear it will disturb the atmosphere of precise calm. "If I want more things, I'll just have to buy another house," she says, not entirely in jest.

Left: Parting gesture. A frosted glass partition visually separates bathroom from bedroom and confers equal importance to each. Frosted glass also conceals the wardrobe. Symbolizing a pool at the foot of a waterfall, the tinted glass wash basin imparts an innocence and, paradoxically, a sensual delight to the daily cleansing routine. Mounting the basin on a pedestal adds a sense of ceremony. Duvet from Heal's, London; cotton sheets from Chinatown, Singapore.

Above left and right: A series of black and white works by Vietnamese photographer Tai and wooden bar stools offer some relief from the severity of the rest of the kitchen, which features a plain concrete floor and stainless steel work surfaces and accessories. Frosted glass windows (unseen) conceal an unsightly view of the opposite building.

Opposite: Back to the future. The owner suggested this modern take on the Japanese tradition of sitting on the floor to maintain the living room's clean lines. "With underside lighting, the sunken sitting area creates an intimate ambience akin to friends gathering around a pit fire," he notes. Burmese *balau* (chosen for its lack of grain) and two antique water jars from Solo, Indonesia, and northern Thailand provide the only strong colour.

Above: Light show. Shards of sunlight play on the wall, granite paving stones and pebbles outside the house, courtesy of a solid *chenggal* trellis topped with glass.

Empty Promise

A living sculpture celebrating space, light, nature and existence is how the owner sees this ultra-minimalist, three-storey, semi-detached urban dwelling. His brief to architect Chan Soo Khian of SCDA Architects, Singapore, was to create "a place of serenity, free from disorder and pretensions; private yet open; austere yet honest; where nature can be felt but not intimidate".

The brief was derived from three years of research, through books and extensive travel particularly to Kyoto, London and New York. "Of great influence were the temples of Japan and monasteries in Europe," says the owner, who then took two years off work to supervise the construction.

Wherever possible, materials are limited to timber – solid *chenggal* for screens and lattices, and wenge-stained *balau* from Myanmar for tables and the living-room bridge – and ivory-coloured honed sile stone from Italy. Everything was custom-made to ensure that the proportions were as intended; even storage boxes used extensively throughout the house were made by a local Shanghainese carpenter through a traditional method with no nails or glue. Natural light streams through skylights moderated by blinds, trellises, walls and glass, both sandblasted and clear. Overhead artificial lighting was avoided as much as possible, with an emphasis on underside lighting, wall recessed lighting and uplighting. Encased in sandblasted glass with timber louvres at the rear, the house surreally looks like a suspended Japanese rice-paper lantern at night.

Above all, it induces discipline and is spiritually refreshing. "I am quite disciplined by nature but a minimalist house helps to perfect the discipline and make it feel good in the process – like practising yoga in a beautiful natural environment," says the owner.

Right: Walking the plank never felt so good as when the plank is a 4.2-m x 1.2-m (13-ft x 4-ft) solid block carved from a single tree, as in this bridge of *balau* wood from Myanmar (foreground) which leads to the cantilevered stairs. At the other end of the living room is a high-walled front courtyard, separated by frameless sliding glass panels, so there is no distinction between outdoors and indoors. This quiet extension of the living area has its own strip of water and a low solid timber bench (mirroring inside elements). Landscaping is kept simple with loose pebbles and a single row of leopard trees, from South America, on either side. "The bark sheds leaving slender trunks spotted with irregular white patches, blending in perfectly with the white surrounding walls and compressed stone flooring," says the owner. A bamboo blind can be seen to the right.

Above left: Nerves of steel. The barely there, thin steel banister was a compromise between the owner (who wanted no railings) and the safety-conscious architect. The stairs lead to the second floor which has two bedrooms linked by a tatami mat meditation room, and a stunning four-sided glass patio overlooking the lower levels.

Above right: Still water. The serenity of the L-shaped pond is accentuated by a lack of fountains.

Far left: Boxing clever. In the living room, three large, custom-made teak boxes store everything needed, a concept borrowed from old Chinese and Japanese houses.

Left: Shades of grey. Jim Thompson raw silk cushions – in off-white, greyish white and light grey – add texture to the sofas. The sunken pit was proportioned to accommodate the coffee table, a 4-m (13-ft) long antique piece of chickenwing timber from an opium bed.

Above: A kitchen worktop in walnut is a warm contrast to the stainless steel appliances and cabinets in silver lacquer by Toncelli, an architecture-trained Italian kitchen cabinet maker whose products are carried by Eurokitchen, Singapore.

Above right: Twist of fête. When observed from the main entrance, the spiral staircase between the second and third storeys looks like a suspended sculpture.

Right: Requiring eight men to lift, the kitchen table (complemented by dining chairs by Capellini in wenge), a continuation of the kitchen worktop, was custom made from solid hardwood in simple straight lines. "Guests feel more relaxed dining in the kitchen while I am preparing food," says the owner of his decision not to have a dedicated dining room – a growing trend.

Left: Chosen to weather like the dark timber in old Japanese houses, *balau* louvres surround the third-storey studio. The desk has an antique timber top which, like the living-room coffee table, was salvaged from an opium bed and modernized with slim stainless steel legs to complement the modern chairs by Capellini in wenge.

Top and above: Living art. Like the ever-changing shadows cast by screens on the walls, wavering water grass in a glass tank removes the need for conventional art in an open-air patio beside the studio, which features a B&B Italia sofa and Jim Thompson silk cushions.

Above: Solitary refinement. Styled like the roll-away mattresses used in Eastern sleeping, the master bed is actually a Western mattress sunken into a raised timber platform, ensuring comfort is not compromised. It is dressed with luxurious white Egyptian cotton.

Right: Custom-made boxes store bedroom paraphernalia including the television and music systems.

Far right: Private screening. A low wall ensures privacy between the bedroom and bathroom behind without reducing air and light flow. There are no doors and the opening is much larger than a standard door width.

Above left and left: Simply beautiful. Philippe Starck-designed bathroom fittings by Duravit and carefully chosen toiletries attest that attention to detail is everything in such a minimalist home. The stone-floored powder room (unseen) on the first floor has an even more Cistercian feel, with an oversized stone cube suspended from the wall just above a stream of water extending from the internal pond. A single spout from the wall acts as a tap.

Above: All a-board. Solid *chenggal* timber decking – as in the rest of the upstairs areas but with gaps between the planks to facilitate drainage – is an unusual yet beautiful option in the bathroom. "I thought if they can do it on boats, they can do it in the bathroom," laughs the owner. Black bamboo, chosen to blend with the dark decking, grows in an open-to-the-air section at right. "The rain does come in, enabling one to be sensitive to nature but without inconvenience."

Opposite: Neutral ground. Soft furnishings in the living room were deliberately chosen to add texture not colour to the predominantly white and wood space. The Frighetto dining chairs are upholstered in stain-resistant fabric while the 'flex-form' sofa set is slip-covered. Asian accents include tasselled Vietnamese boxes covered with burnt duck-egg shell (Tarahome) containing organdie napkins from India (Tarahome); Australian-made Room stainless-steel bowls and chopsticks (Lifestorey); a *jedi* basket, woven from water hyacinth in the Philippines (The Lifeshop); and on the coffee table lemongrass, lychee and *cempaka*-scented candles made in Hong Kong (Tarahome).

Screen Play

Essentially two boxes defined by sliding and pivoting screens, this three-storey house is a 'dematerialized' zone in which surfaces are not quite what they seem. Tempering the intense sun are screens and lattices that mediate and differentiate between interior and exterior spaces. Walls slide apart and overlap each other, or, as in the detached frontal wall, and the ceiling-height partition dividing the living area from the kitchen, are open at each end to encourage a free flow of traffic and light. Water also flows from the external *koi* pond under the detached front wall into the powder rooms. Even obtrusive columns are eliminated by integrating the window mullions into the structural system of the house.

Owner Lee Mon Sun and his wife Wy-Mann originally wanted a Balinese resort-style design. They were persuaded by Chan Soo Khian of SCDA Architects to transcend traditional imagery in favour of a more contemporary language and an abstract, stream-lined look which fulfilled their desire for a minimalist living space. "Whilst modern in spirit, the design and materials are organic in their inception," says Soo Khian. "What is important is the desire to create organized and controlled spaces that can affect the human spirit."

The simple palette of construction materials (off-form concrete, stained plywood cladding, steel-framed Bondeck floors, yellow granite from China and *chenggal* timber screens, one of which is motorized and amounts to half the width of the rear elevation) is mirrored in the furnishings and accessories, which are kept to a minimum. "We have lived through clutter as a lifestyle and find less is more fun now," notes Mon. Indeed, material assets take second place to this ethereal and carefully choreographed series of spaces.

Above: The slatted timber underside of the entertainment pavilion acts as a partial ceiling to the deck area. Thai raw silk bolsters (The Lifeshop) recline on teak deckchairs. In the background, two Ming-style chairs flank a camphorwood table – the only family heirlooms displayed in the house. "We wanted something overtly Asian to represent where we are," says Mon. The staircase to the pavilion – which is suspended on steel posts so that it floats over the deck area and pool – is reached through the slatted wooden door, back right. The pavilion acts as a lightweight counterpoint to the heavy-weight 'box' of the main house.

Left: Back to basics. A simple low seating arrangement in teak offset with white PVC cushions is perfect for the cubic entertainment pavilion – and can be moved when the Lees' two young sons want to play. The *chenggal* louvres are adjustable by hand. 'Jing' table and platform, chopsticks and flatware *(above),* all made in Thailand, are from The Lifeshop. *Cempaka-* and green tea-scented candles on mango wood bases are from Tarahome, Singapore.

Left: Blind love. Moderating the fierce equatorial light, off-white cotton blinds give a veiled, translucent quality to the living room. The floor is honed limestone.

Opposite, clockwise from top left: Eastern flavours: *jedi* water-hyacinth basket from the Philippines (The Lifeshop) makes a rustic magazine receptacle; Indian organdie napkins (Tarahome) on the dining table; in the marble and metal kitchen a *capiz* shell salad bowl from the Philippines (Tarahome) is an organic counterpoint to modern Mono salad servers and Zac salt and pepper mills (both from Germany at Lifestorey); unobtrusive modern lighting imparts a candle-like glow above the dining table; underlining the house's earthy textures and shades are kitchen spices such as cumin, cardamom and paprika (Wire-works, London at Lifestorey); tasselled Vietnamese box coated with burnt duck-egg shell (Tarahome).

Far left: Detached feeling. Animating the stairwell, light floods in through slot windows in the detached concrete frontal wall. Glass, steel, wood and concrete give the area a feeling of installation art.

Left: Sunken treasure. The pure pleasure of a sunken bath, designed in sile stone by Soo Khian, is heightened by the simplicity of the glass and wood surroundings. Rice and aloe bath oils from Hong Kong (The Lifeshop) and a *capiz* shell soap dish from the Philippines (Tarahome) are luxurious touches. Soo Khian also designed the study's L-shaped desk in stainless steel (for the side supporting the computer) and walnut (main table), with a concrete base (unseen).

Opposite: Fringe benefits. A fringed jute bedcover and cushions and knitted cotton cardigan throw, all made in India, are homely influences in the spartan master bedroom, where even the bedside tables are incorporated into the custom-made bed head. The entertainment pavilion can be seen across the glass-bordered outdoor walkway through the window on the left, while the frosted glass window of the *en suite* bathroom appears through the doorway on the right. The motorized slatted timber screen acts as a veil to the master bedroom and adjacent study. Bed linen except for the waffle-weave pillowcases by Charlie Brown, Australia (Lifestorey) and accessories such as the Vietnamese duck eggshell boxes in the bed head shelves are from Tarahome. The floor is African golden teak.

Right: Punched with holes, this weathered *chenggal*-wood stool stands sentry over the *koi* pond at the front entrance, just inside the imposing solid yellow granite wall. In contrast to the private frontage, the back visage is characterized by full-height glass screens.

Far right: Carved from a solid block of granite, this elongated wash basin is a new take on the more traditional 'his' and 'her' basins. A key board (Zac, Germany at Lifestorey) holds jewellery next to a gleaming *capiz* shell cotton-wool container made in the Philippines (TaraHome).

Sliding Doors

Inspired by Southeast Asia's 'buildings without walls' and the flow of spaces in Japanese dwellings, Chris White began renovating his newly bought apartment by knocking down anything extraneous. This included kitchen walls, the original staircase and the glazing on the roof terrace. "I wanted to create a flexible, spacious, yet beautiful environment in which to live," recalls the English architect/interior designer.

Captivated by the philosophy behind contemporary five-star Asian resort hotels such as the Aman chain, he set out to capture – elegantly and luxuriously – local ways of living and being open to the elements. A prerequisite for the purchase was the fourth-floor roof terrace, now landscaped with tight granite-tiled planters filled with strictly green and white tropicals.

Apart from the oversized solid oak front door, there are no hinged doors on the premises – only sliding frosted glass screens suggestive of Japanese *fusama*. Careful furniture groupings and different levels rather than conventional walls demarcate the living areas in the open-plan interior, reminiscent of a New York loft. High-end minimalist detailing using natural materials such as slate and solid timber, as in the works of contemporary Western designers David Chipperfield and John Pawson, and a limited palette of colours, completed the transformation.

Above: On the roof terrace, tread-boards from the original staircase rest on a concrete-covered brick base to create a table surrounded by metallic chairs from a Spanish café. A miniature pond with a black glazed water jar from China fills an awkward space between two columns.

Right: The dining area, like the whole of the apartment, is a deceptively simple balance of the five Asian elements (fire, metal, stone, wood and water). Two hand-made beaten steel candlesticks from Thailand – which took more than a year to deliver – are on the oak console, designed by Chris.

Right: Black magic. Practical, masculine and stylish, black and its close counterpart, charcoal grey, is the main colour accent in the living and dining areas. They are seen here from the kitchen, a continuation of the downstairs space, where all opportunities for clutter, including the dish rack and refrigerator, are concealed and even the wine rack is recessed. Chris designed the stainless-steel table in the foreground, on which rests a futuristic glass dish (Potterhaus Singapore).

Far left: Below the oak stairs to the reading room, a Chinese 'moongate' is an ideal platform for a vase. Halogen spotlights are strategically positioned to highlight features such as these. The auspicious shape is echoed in the external moongate in the terrace wall.

Left: Mao and zen. At the head of the frosted glass dining table, a Chairman Mao print was originally intended for a Chinese fusion restaurant designed by Chris's friend and fellow architect Ed Poole. A Balinese palm leaf container finished in silver (Pagoda House Gallery) rests on the oak-based table designed by Chris.

Opposite, clockwise from top left: Dreamlining: stainless steel work surfaces are an attractive foil to oak-finished cupboards in the kitchen, where a 1950s Vola tap is an elegant touch; hand-beaten steel chopsticks from Thailand in a glass dish (Potterhaus Singapore); on the extended mezzanine level now used as a reading/television room, a heavy Balinese mortar is one of several used as candlebases, plant pots, ashtrays or decorative objects in their own right (a limited edition print by contemporary British artist Bridget Reilly injects a rare colour accent below); a wall hanging of old bamboo scrolls from a Burmese temple mounted on silk continues the black and wood theme near the master bedroom; Chris's version of a Chinese opium bed lies below four antique mirrors from a Chinese medicine shop in the reading room; buffalo-horn beakers on a simple tray (all from Club 21 Gallery) on the coffee table.

Right: Successful pitch. Partly inspired by New York loft living, the open plan of the apartment works vertically as well as horizontally. Opening up the pitched ceiling made room for the upstairs master bedroom, top left, while enclosing the verandah allowed for a dining area (partly seen on right) which flows on from the living area. Designed by Chris, the charcoal-coloured sofa and daybed, together with two 'club chairs' in rattan (Fong Brothers, Singapore), encircle an oak coffee table conveniently on castors, also designed by Chris. A 1930s Modigliani print hangs above the sofa. The lamps are from Heal's, London.

Right: Flimsy excuse. A daringly minimal steel and oak handrail separates the master bedroom and the downstairs living area. The barely there balustrading continues on the staircase, which features the same handrail and treads that seem to float on layers of light. One of two temple rubbings from Angkor Wat, Cambodia behind the bed can be seen by the full-length mirror, which rests simply against the wall. Chris designed the glass-topped oak bedside table cabinets. Wool rug from IKEA. Waffle-weave white cotton kimono from Mara Miri, Singapore.

Above left: A frosted glass sliding door separates the bedroom from the bathroom, which features an old oversized porcelain basin from a chemical shop, Philippe Starck chrome fixtures and black Indian slate. "There is nothing better than lying in the bath with the door open to the small garden and stars above," says Chris.

Above right: Chris does much of his work from his home office, on the wall of which is a print of a piece by US artist Mark Rothko.

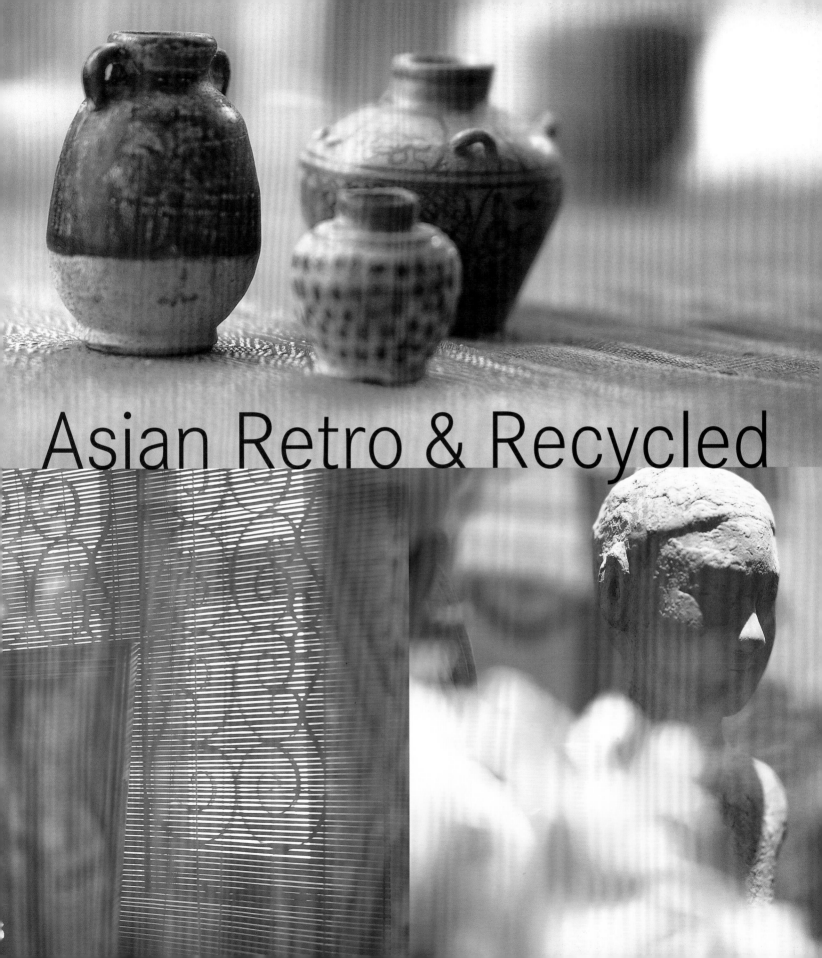

Asian Retro & Recycled

Opposite: The colour purple. Green and purple bulbs from a Salvation Army thrift shop glisten like grapes in a Khmer offering bowl in a late-Qing Dynasty blackwood altar table. A fuchsia chenille throw (IKEA) and cushion covers with a chinoiserie design (Schumacher, US) accessorize a rattan sofa upholstered in lavender-hued rough cotton. In the left-hand corner stands a gilded decorative piece from Cambodia.

Finishing Touches

The lightness of lime and lilac on an antique altar. Hawker-stall memories and hand-painted finishes. Thai silk and tassels. Style in this seaside apartment has more to do with improvization than affluence.

Raffles International art services manager Arabella Richardson says of her vibrant colour scheme: "This particular hue of purple, a lilac, helps reduce the glare and also changes with the light at different times of the day, turning pink if there is a good sunset. Lime green accents are tropical and contrasting."

A two-toned lilac pinstriped wall turns a long awkward corridor into a feature in itself. On one side of the corridor, a mid-Qing Dynasty blackwood altar table supports carefully selected but casually assembled Southeast Asian treasures. On the other, a series of precisely placed personal photographs forms an intriguing gallery. Framed works by London-based photographer and friend Russell Wright — whose subjects include a durian and a Doc Martin boot — are cost-effective alternatives to more conventional art.

The fine art/art history graduate with training in decorative paint finishing designed the coffee table, applied its creamy, crackled gold finish and handpainted frangipani and dragonflies onto the glass-encased calico centre. A tortoise-shell paint finish, also hand-done, enlivens the once plain wooden dining table.

Recycled elements are quirky counterpoints to Chinese antiques and designer artificial floral arrangements. A pair of timber corner cornices from India delineate the dining and living spaces; a wooden cutting block from a chicken-rice hawker stall on a custom-made base provides additional workspace in the kitchen; ceramic shophouse balustrades now bear candles on the balcony. A second-hand aluminium water heater tank supports an old marble tabletop from a Chinese coffee-shop, on which sits a decorative lotus-bud finial in weathered cement from Phnom Penh. A brass wine bucket and stand were originally from a club in Geylang, Singapore's red-light district.

The use of recycled and personally made pieces is budget-friendly and individualizes the décor. Arabella's trademark use of colour and eclectic combination of old and new accessories, furniture, fabrics and artwork further personalize this elegant interior.

Above: Flooded with natural light on two sides, the living area flows onto a broad balcony overlooking the sea. Bamboo chicks spray-painted white can be let down to mitigate the midday sun.

Far left: Thai silk bolsters with antique bone buttons rest upon three Filipino rattan storage baskets. Other fabric accents (unseen) include raffia tassels (Houles, France) which add finesse to simple bamboo blinds.

Left: A lacquered offering vessel from Sukhothai, silver candlesticks from India, silver incense holders shaped like melons from Phnom Penh and an artificial orchid (Studio 78) adorn a mid-Qing Dynasty blackwood altar table in the hall. "I tread the fine line between too much and too little, professionally and personally," notes their owner. "The important thing is to work with the environment, not against it."

Opposite: Tea and tortoise-shell. A glamorous finish on an inexpensive dining table and an eclectic ensemble of flatware including *famille rose* china and limited-edition Lynn Chase underline Arabella's assertion that she is "definitely not a matching person".

Right: A wooden chopping block from a hawker stall has cutting-edge appeal.

Far right: Monkey business. A Jim Thompson Thai silk scarf with a monkey motif makes a whimsical wine towel on this second-hand champagne bucket and stand. In the background are sandstone balls (Rainforest Shop, Singapore).

Opposite: In the stunning turquoise-painted bedroom, an antique iron four poster bed spray-painted white is draped with embroidered white cotton linen (Yue Hwa Department Store, Singapore). An unusual dragon *galae* (finial) from Thailand and an orchid arrangement (Studio 78) grace the self-assembled bedside table from IKEA. In a corner is a mahogany Victorian lady's chair (unseen), reupholstered in what was once a *faux* leopard fur jacket.

Right: Purple passage. A pinstriped wall is the backdrop to a stunning artificial Phaleonopsis orchid from Studio 78, Singapore. To the right, thick, white-washed frames (IKEA) lend a 'peep-hole' effect to old family photographs.

Far left: Plentiful in Chinatown markets, this *kamcheng* (lidded) bowl brightens up the tiny bathroom.

Left: The feathery caress of a boa on a reproduction Louis chair from Indonesia, upholstered in a Warner's damask fabric, heightens the corridor's feminine flavour.

Opposite: The largest pieces in the living room are two ancestor paintings, one of which is at the back of the marble-inlaid rosewood Chinese bench, a 100-year-old collector's piece given to Ernesto by a client. A watercolour of a mountain landscape, *The Window,* by Chinese artist Susan Wong is on the left. A full-length mirror near the front door visually elongates the space.

Right: Eyrie feeling. The guest room, a suspended stage formed by demolishing the ceiling, is reached by a spindly steel stepladder.

Artistic Licence

In delightful contrast to the tropical modern abodes he designs for Southeast Asia's élite, the inner-city apartment tenanted by architect Ernesto Bedmar is unassuming and highly personal. As such, it is a privilege to enter his home of 18 years.

"It's not a designer place," he says of the two-bedroom, government-owned flat. "But it is authentic, it's comfortable; it's me; filled with things I have been collecting over the years."

The walls of his living room serve as a gallery for the small but outstanding art collection which Ernesto has assembled over two decades of living in Asia. These include mixed-media paintings from China, Sri Lanka, Singapore (including a provocative early Jimmy Ong) and India which cover most of the limited wall space (so limited, in fact, that Ernesto built a high, narrow wall on which to hang one of his ancestor paintings).

After plans to extend the space horizontally by acquiring the neighbouring apartment fell through, Ernesto decided that the only way to go was up. With typical aplomb, he removed the low ceiling, reclaiming

at least another six metres (20 ft) of vertical space in the living and dining areas and carving out a raised concrete platform on which now rests, rather precariously, a guest bed.

Asked what sort of house he would design for himself, the genius behind masterpieces such as the Khattar House (see page 30) and The Leedon Park Limited Edition Series, says he would prefer to alter or enlarge an old house with a history behind it. "It is too much of a responsibility to design a house for myself," concedes the man who chooses to sleep on a simple mattress on the floor.

Opposite, clockwise from top left: **Democracy**, by Singapore artist Vincent Leow, hangs on one wall of the living room (a wooden horse puppet from Myanmar with articulated limbs rests below); Ernesto added a high, narrow wall for his latest acquisition, an exquisitely detailed antique painting on cloth depicting a Chinese couple's transition to the afterlife; a simple pod on the coffee table, an original Thai teak table covered with an opium mat; eschewing a closet, Ernesto's workwear hangs on racks in a corner of the master bedroom, while his shoes stand to attention in formation on the parquet floor (unseen); the black-painted bathroom with gilded accents; items like socks are stored in a magnificent Chinese medicine chest.

Right: Faced with limited space, Ernesto enclosed the balcony, transforming it into a dining recess off the living room. On the wall behind the simple glass table rest two temple pillars from India; on the console, a Burmese papier mâché box in the shape of a chicken.

Left: A painting of an old abandoned dance room by a young artist from northern Thailand leans against the wall at the head of the master bed, which is a simple, almost monastic, mattress on the floor. In the corner is a Ming-style rosewood chair.

Opposite: Like much of the architect's work, which includes Singapore's Ridley Park House, the Eu Houses I and II, Residence 8 and the Glencairn Residence, Ernesto's tongue-in-cheek entry to a regional fashion event was a sensation. The figure presides over the purely utilitarian kitchen which did not, however, escape Ernesto's penchant for spotlighting.

Filial Factor

When four adult brothers – each brilliant with individual tastes developed from years of living overseas – decide to build a house in which to live with their parents, the architectural brief could be a little daunting. "It was like having five or six sets of clients," recalls Justin Hill of Kerry Hill Architects (KHA), Singapore, which had worked on two other projects for the family. "Dick is into pop, Peter is interested in family history, John wanted a comfortable space for treasured things, Wah wanted a working space for his photography, Mrs (Elizabeth) Lee is a gourmet cook and Mr (Kip Lee) Lee is a noted historian and book collector."

Impressed with the clean, contemporary lines and natural materials of the KHA-designed, five-star Datai resort in Langkawi, Malaysia, the family asked KHA to design a house with separate sections for each member on the site of their previous home. The latter had been built in 1958 in a jungle area of Bukit Timah dotted with farms and quiet *kampongs*. "By the early 1990s, we were all returning to Singapore from our studies overseas and the house was inadequate for our needs," notes Peter, the second youngest son and chief coordinator with KHA. "We had always enjoyed living together and had many important memories and attachments to the place. In terms of feng shui, the land is almost ideal, having a north-south axis and a slope."

Above: The broad hallway between the front door and dining room is light and airy, with a honed limestone floor. The imposing oil paintings of the Lees' ancestors, including the sons' great grandmother Koh Gim Tien (1855–1940), the daughter of Koh Eng Hoon (1823–1880), one of Singapore's pioneers, were done in Beijing.

Left: Coming clean. A custom-made, cast-concrete tub in Wah's 'zen' bathroom needs no further adornment than a solitary plant.

Right: A late 19th-century polychrome enamelled *kam-cheng* (lidded) porcelain bowl sits before an early 20th-century Peranakan carved teak mirror with gold leaf in the family room. The well-used Steinway is reflected.

Below: An antique Sino-Javanese wood lamp stand, a bronze candlestand, a 1970s Thai teak fruit bowl and porcelain teacups from Taiwan rest on the elmwood and black lacquered altar table in Peter's sitting room. Peter is an art consultant on such cutting-edge projects as The Straits Club at the Fullerton Hotel, Singapore.

Although the full-length glass windows in the communal areas usher in light and green views, and water features including ponds and a 25-m (80-ft) pool are incorporated, the U-shaped house is essentially inward-looking. So too is its emphasis on the occupants' shared history and on time-honoured Asian values. Sepia-tinged family photos are evident in every room. Recessed alcoves similar to Japanese *tokonama* in the hall in the parents' wing contain century-old Nonya artefacts including a collection of gilded offering boxes. The entrance hall is lined with oil paintings of ancestors, many of whom were so prominent politically and socially that they have streets in Singapore named after them. "There are already nine generations of Lees in Singapore," says Peter, a keen geneaologist. "The first, Lee Kan (1760–1844), left Eng Choon district in China's Fujian province for Malacca in 1776."

Uniform architectural and décor details throughout the house such as full-length, *balau*-wood framed glass doors, linen and silk rugs custom made in Belgium, Baleri sofas and customized furniture designed by KHA create a complex yet coherent whole which adroitly satisfies each individual occupant's needs and collections.

Above left: Framed photographs of Dick, John, Peter and Wah on the piano in the family room.

Above right: A *guzheng* (Chinese zither), which Mrs Lee plays.

Opposite: With full-length glass windows on three sides, the dining room has a conservatory feel. Furniture and fittings are in suitably muted shades, including the Spanish dining chairs around the KHA-designed teak dining table, which sits 16 people. An artichoke-shaped lamp by Scandinavian designer Poul Henningsen by Louis Poulsen and figures of *Fu Lu Shou* (the Gods of Prosperity, Emolument and Longevity) on a late Qing dynasty blackwood altar table contribute to a global feel. Flowers by Jo Marais.

Above left: Strong statements. Bought in Beijing by Peter as a gift for his brother, 1970s propaganda posters from China's Cultural Revolution in Dick's sitting room hang above 'Tulip' chairs in fibreglass and aluminium and a table designed by US-based, Finland-born designer Eero Saarinen for Florence Knoll in 1956.

Above right: Show piece. A poster promoting *Fried Rice Paradise,* one of Dick's musicals, complements Thai silk cushion covers in the entertainer's sitting room.

Right: Bought inexpensively at a moving sale and Changi junk shop respectively, the round solid teak dining table and two old teak armchairs minus their arms make a fun dining-room ensemble. The other chairs are antique English balloon-backs, a gift from Callie's mother. A local upholsterer made the skirted seat cushions with fabric from IKEA. The arched window to the kitchen allows the passage of light and food between the rooms.

A Little Romance

Elevating eclecticism to a style in its own right, Callie Peet filled her 1935 East Coast terrace house with recycled Asian pieces and beloved family heirlooms. "I don't care for modern or ordinary furniture that has no character and is strictly functional," says the Minnesota-born graphic designer/artist who lived in Singapore for four years. "I like old things with a sense of history and romance. And I have a sense of humour and adventure; I like my rooms to look fun."

Chinese, Indonesian, Tibetan, Balinese and French furniture and accessories merged in this quirky, comfortable oasis which seemed somehow removed from everyday ugliness. Callie replaced all the fluorescent bulbs with low lighting and kept rubbish bins and anything plastic out of sight, for instance. "I also love warm, rich colours and am not afraid of having many colours in one room," notes the ceramic artist who is inspired by sojourns in Asia, Italy and Mexico.

While traditional architecture blessed the interior with tall ceilings for ventilation and charming French-style double wood doors, it omitted built-in closets or any sort of storage space. Callie turned this to her advantage by collecting cabinets of all shapes, sizes and colours. Three lacquered reproduction Chinese wedding cabinets – green, yellow and red – act as a kitchen pantry, television and stereo cupboard and linen closet respectively. One of these, an old teak and glass display case in which its former owners had kept clothes, became her tableware cabinet. "When you have things you love, that are beautiful and fun, it's a waste to keep them where they can't be seen and enjoyed," she says.

Most of her pieces continue to 'work' back in the US, where she now lives in a log cabin at the base of the Rocky Mountains. Callie managed to sell her former gardening cupboard, an old *wayang kulit* puppet cabinet, to a doctor "for a lot more than I paid for it". "It now sits in her waiting room and contains extra medical supplies." And the crockery cabinet? "I had that made into two separate pieces – there is no way it would fit in your standard American home, the ceilings aren't tall enough."

Opposite, clockwise from top left: A miniature Thai temple and Parisian lamps on top of a Chinese yellow wedding cabinet; next to an old elm and bamboo altar table (Just Anthony) in the dining room are three Vietnamese lacquered containers which a groom-to-be is required to present full of food to the bride's family before a wedding; a sandalwood Buddha sits on a window-sill by the front door in the living room "keeping peace over the whole house"; a ceramic monkey, made in China, holds a dish containing a candle and berries; Thai puppets bought for S$8 each at Bangkok's weekend market hang near the front door; an old lithograph collected by Callie's grandfather during World War II, advertizing a railroad trip in France, hangs above a hand-carved minibar cabinet from Thailand on which rests an inexpensive Chinese teapot.

Right: Across from the living-room sofa, a composition of treasured objects invites restful contemplation: a piece of handwoven silk from Cambodia; a Balinese hat; an antique carved wooden angel from Bali; a 19th-century Tibetan cabinet (Lopburi, Singapore); and a little teak table from a shop in Dempsey Road, Singapore.

Left: In the living room, a 19th-century, hand-painted cabinet from Tibet serves as an 'open bar', supporting bottles and bar accessories including vintage Singapore glasses for Tiger Beer and Kickapoo Joy Juice. Sepia-tone photographs of Callie's grandmother and her brother taken in 1908 in St Paul, Minnesota hang above.

Opposite: Recurring theme. Two small pictures of Chinese wedding cabinets and a Chinese scroll painting, one of three purchased for a song from a street vendor at Chinese New Year, hang on the living-room wall.

Far left: Callie made these striking cushion covers from narrow bolts of inexpensive blue and white cotton fabric common in Shanghai.

Left: A dynamic contrast to the red wall, a yellow lacquered Chinese wedding cabinet from Just Anthony, Singapore, contains laser discs and other entertainment accessories in the living room. A Chinese teapot from Thow Kwang Industries, Singapore makes a fun vase.

Right: Case study. A teak and glass display case from an old laundry showcases crockery and glassware. "I loved arranging my treasures inside that glass cabinet, it was sort of an art project for me," recalls Callie.

Above left: In a corner of the dining room, festive Balinese umbrellas are arranged like flowers in an urn. In the archway separating dining room and kitchen, three Thai-style domed ceramic jars, bought at Chatuchak Weekend Market in Bangkok, contain small kitchen items such as tea bags.

Left: An old wooden wine box (from Asia Passion along Dempsey Road, Singapore) stores kitchen utensils.

Above: Pot-pourri. Enamel pots from a French fleamarket hang from a rack, above which sit colourful round trays ("always cheap and great to take to parties as they don't break") from Singapore, Thailand and Vietnam. An avid cook, Callie loved the large and sunny kitchen that had ample wall space for her enamelware and other kitchenware. "Almost the entire ceiling opened up using a corrugated plastic sliding roof system," she recalls. "Once I left it open when it rained – which happens suddenly in Asia – and that was rather exciting."

Left: Opposite the bed, a Chinese elm medicine chest, from Just Anthony, conceals a small television in its top cabinet. Purchased from an antique shop in Malacca, Malaysia, rustic baskets – originally used to carry food to Chinese weddings – store belts and scarves.

Below: An Indian-made cotton bedspread, bought in Paris, and Italian cushion covers from The Link Home, Singapore, dress a handmade pinewood bed from Jackson, Wyoming. "My bedroom is a place of peace and rest so I don't like it to be cluttered with too much visual stimuli," says Callie. "The oil painting behind the bed was done by a Colorado artist. I bought it before I moved to Singapore to remind me of the vast open spaces of the Western United States."

Opposite, clockwise from top left: In the upstairs hallway off the bedroom, rice baskets made of lacquered, woven bamboo, bought for S$25 each at Bangkok's weekend market, "would make great fat lamp bases", muses Callie; treasured books rest on simple wicker baskets (IKEA) at the end of the bed; a small handpainted chest from India sits next to the Chinese medicine cabinet in the bedroom; a watering can used to tend ferns sits on the ledge of the covered walkway to the master bathroom; offering baskets bought from a small *warung* (roadside store) in Bali, used to carry food to the temple, sit in a corner of the stair-way; a straw mat sourced in Hanoi defines the open-to-the-elements walkway, which gives the upstairs bathroom a sense of being outside.

New Asian Accents

Clockwise from left: Let there be light. A traditional Peranakan lampshade (Tong Mern Sern Antiques, Arts and Crafts) in Arabella Richardson's apartment; assembled in Indonesia, standing bamboo and Indian cotton lights look great in multiples marching up stairs as here, or singly in a corner (Mara Miri); Tibetan prayer bells rest beside a lamp base made from an old blue and white Chinese ginger jar (Callie Peet).

Bright Ideas

From rattan fish-traps to ceramic ginger jars, creamy *capiz* shell to delicate rice paper, the décor world is switching on to exotic lighting options. Antique and recycled shades and bases are beautifying the bulb (hidden altogether in many minimalist and modern homes), while sculptural designs (from Isamu Noguchi's organic minimal masterpieces to Mara Miri's tribal bamboo 'torches') mean feature lights are standing up for themselves. Trellises, screens and translucent materials dissect and diffuse natural light, defining living spaces and imbuing them with an ever-changing ambience. And with renewed emphasis on holistic homes, candles continue to be a source of enlightenment: scented with sandalwood or cinnamon, multiwicked and magnificent, or simply tealights sitting in a stone tray.

Clockwise from top right: Light relief. Handmade wrought-iron and rice-paper candle stands are mounted in granite bases (Cynosure Design) (the wooden lamp-shades in the background are Czech) in Johnny Tan's house; a 1920s surgical lamp purchased in New York for its "sexy lines" in an Asian art-deco interior; threaded with colourful Indian cotton, rattan fish-trap baskets from Vietnam make exotic light shades (Mara Miri); a silver candlestick from Malacca is updated with a lime-coloured candle (Arabella Richardson); a nine-wick candle from Thailand on a handbeaten iron and compacted plywood stand (Banyan Tree Gallery).

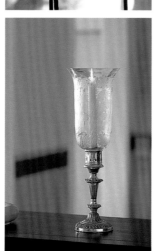

Clockwise from left: Gardens of Paradise. Smooth river stones *(left)* or coarse granite slabs *(right,* by Stephen Caffyn) punctuate pathways; a volcanic andesite Buddha from Yogjakarta at the foot of a banyan tree in Claire Chiang's garden; an Indonesian *balau* bridge, pebble stone pond, Italian stone feature wall and clear polycarbonate sheet roof from Johnny Tan's modern conservatory (Cynosure Design); utilitarian objects made of humble materials, such as this Japanese bamboo water scoop or *hishaku,* work well in minimalist modern spaces (the Tongs); undeterred by the petite parameters of his front garden, Sim Chen-Min of eco-id designed this stylish treehouse in aluminium and *chenggal,* with a parachute for a roof, for his three-year-old daughter Linnet.

Outside Influence

Be it a *siheyuan* (Chinese house with a central court-yard) or *sala* (Thai open pavilion), *pendopo* (central pavilion in Javanese houses) or *balé* (Balinese thatched-roof platform), traditional Asian living spaces have embraced gardens and water features for centuries. Living with nature continues to be seen as vital for well-being in sophisticated cities such as Singapore where the floor space allowed for apartments was recently increased to encourage the building of 'gardens in the sky'. Eco-architecture is the latest buzzword, with landscaping dictating not only the bits in between buildings but the structure and façades of buildings themselves. From minimalist 'pebble ponds' and lap pools (placed indoors as well as out) to rustic water jars and statuary, exotic outdoor features are anything but garden-variety.

Clockwise from above left: A moat-like pond features granite stepping stones, water jars from Indonesia and heavy iron chains to channel rainwater (Guz Wilkinson Architects); small wooden boxes such as this one hanging from a hybrid guava enlarge the planting area available in Sim Chen-Min's small garden; a hardy tropical succulent; a bas-relief from Yogjakarta (Claire Chiang); grass makes an impact in a glazed cobalt pot (Sim Chen-Min).

Clockwise from right: Fruitful labour. Featuring tropical fruit and flowers, an arrangement by Singapore-based Jo Marais who studied with Paula Pryke in London, on an heirloom rosewood pedestal table, in the Lees' family home; yellow orchids in a lontar palm container (Judy McGrath); another composition by Jo Marais; white lotuses – symbolic of Buddhism and purity in Asia – collected at dawn from a Chinese temple are arranged in a Thai green celadon pot; this 'naturalistic' arrangement is characteristic of Cecilia Ng Lay Kuan of Woodsville Florist, Singapore.

Natural Instincts

From a single blossom behind a Buddha's ear through the studied poetry of Japanese ikebana to Thailand's ornate *krathong* arrangements, floral adornment comes naturally in Asia. While the graceful potted orchid plant has become endemic to interiors across the globe, fresh ideas include home-grown foliage and flowers (think heliconias, birds of paradise or arum lilies) casually composed in or out of interesting containers (such as a brushed steel bowl, a wooden wine crate or a Burmese offering tray). Another offshoot involves bounty plucked from the kitchen – fruit, vegetables, herbs, spices and grains. Layers of different coloured rices look fabulous in a glass vase, while chilli peppers or mandarins add exotic interest when mixed with greenery. Experimenting with humble twigs, weeds, mosses and grasses (including spiralling bamboo or spindly branches) is also popular. And with busier, more environmentally sensitive lifestyles, there is artificial intelligence in the use of convincing (and cost-effective) *faux* arrangements. Take your pick.

Clockwise from top left: A coconut-shaped pot from Chiang Mai contains a glory lily *(Gloriosa superba)* in Stanley Tan's sile stone bathroom; angular bird of paradise blooms in a Thai pot (Catherine LaJeunesse); a single frangipani in a 'corpuscle' dish (Blue Canopy) on Arabella Richardson's altar table; artificial lotuses adorn a mirrored bamboo antique offering stand from Laos (Ramona Galardi); a dried lotus pod is displayed in a celadon vase in the Tongs' home.

Clockwise from right: A lamp-base made from a Filipino basket (Isabel Mendezona); a gilded 19th-century Burmese carving of 'Garuda biting a Naga' complements the honeyed tones of a 19th-century Chinese partners' desk and 'horseshoe' chairs in elm (Catherine LaJeunesse); a wooden carving symbolizing a closed lotus from Chiang Mai, Thailand (Claire Chiang); sculptural starfruit in a lacquered offering tray from Myanmar; an old carving from Kalimantan surveys a sophisticated dining-table setting, complete with rattan place mats from Bali (Catherine LaJeunesse).

Wood Works

A traditional tropical building and craft material, wood welcomes like no other element. Yet in this age of diminishing hardwood resources, its continued use in construction goes against the grain. Increasingly recycled and restricted to architectural detailing or replaced altogether by less-endangered materials like bamboo and coconut palm, wood and related 'living' elements have never been more popular as accent pieces. Furniture ranges in hue from bleached or brushed oak (no lightweight in modern homes) through richly textured *huanghuali* (dating from the Chinese Ming and Qing Dynasties) to chocolate-brown teak (an Indonesian evergreen). Composite woods and surface treatments such as wenge now offer a veneer of respectability. Water hyacinth, pandanus, palmyra, rattan, jute and other fibrous reeds weave warmth into home accessories such as baskets, boxes, cushion covers, screens, lamp shades and bases. Primitive carvings impart texture to refined interiors while lacquerware lends gloss to rustic settings.

Clockwise from above right: Pandora's boxes. A mother-of-pearl inlaid box for storing betel-chewing equipment from Vietnam, lacquered containers shaped as stylized durians from Sumatra and an old Burmese silver container on Judy McGrath's coffee table; lacquerware such as this square dish from Myanmar (the Tongs) relies on the oil of the lacquer tree and centuries-old craftsmanship; lacquered Burmese offering containers and a pumpkin-shaped box on an Indian-daybed coffee table; a Burmese offering container (*hsun-ok*) rests on Sim Chen-Min's dining table made from two 2.5-m (8-ft) long teak planks on steel legs.

This page, clockwise from right: Set against modern mixed-media pieces, a Burmese alabaster Guanyin graces a Thai rain drum between two Burmese monks' alms bowls (Ramona Galardi); Burmese *hsun-oks* delineate a study (Catherine LaJeunesse); Vietnamese water pots fill a space beneath an antique Chinese side table, behind which a late-19th-century Chinese cabinet supports Burmese *hsun-oks*; Cambodian betel-nut boxes and a Vietnamese mother-of-pearl inlaid box flank gilded Burmese 'travelling' Buddhas on a Chinese rosewood tea stand lying on a Tibetan folding prayer table (Ramona Galardi); an antique Chinese *laohan* (daybed) bears treasures including an 18th-century, Shan-style, lacquered sandstone Burmese Buddha head (Catherine LaJeunesse).

Urges and Acquisitions

Contrary to popular conceptions of zen, the contemplation of objects and the art of display are very much age-old Asian traditions. From seashells to *sake* cups, ceramics to *hsun-oks*, perfume bottles to personal mementoes, beauty (and value) is very much in the eye of the New Asian collector. For maximum impact, differences or similarities between objects may be emphasized by placing them in uniform shelving or clustering them. Each and every living area (including entrances, kitchens and bathrooms) can be enriched by well-chosen *objets-d'art* and imaginative display techniques: hang a tiger rug on the wall or put a Chairman Mao bust outside the front door. For everyday use, if appropriate, use antique Chinese desks and altar tables, Asian art-deco, retro or colonial furniture and exotic receptacles.

Clockwise from far left: Shrine of the times. Collections of spiritual objects, like this Guanyin, Buddha and Cybaba picture, are increasingly popular (Ramona Galardi); an 18th-century Burmese Buddha (generally not as costly as Thai images) sits on an antique Chinese altar table in dealer Catherine LaJeunesse's home; four of more than 170 white Mao Zedong figurines on a teak cabinet collected by a homeowner in Singapore.

Clockwise from right:
Practical magic. Cushions in animal prints and earthy tones complement a scarlet sofa in Isabel Mendezona's lounge; a geometrically patterned Laotian shawl (foreground) draped over an off-white sofa by Franco-Indian interior designer Ramona Galardi; *kilim* saddlebags are revived as cushion covers in Ramona Galardi's lounge; a hand-embroidered throw and cushions from India (Mara Miri) are a sensual touch.

Fabric of Society

Texture talks in today's interiors – indeed, many mavens are calling it 'the new colour' – and one of the surest ways to achieve it is through textiles. Long treasured in Asia as religious and royal artefacts, handcrafted cloths such as *ikat*, batik and silks add finesse to modern furnishings. Picture opulent silk sari cushions on a minimalist sofa; a Thai hill-tribe child's costume against a stark white wall; an Indonesian sarong stretched across a frame in a study. While earth colours like cinnamon and ash are softly subtle, catwalk colours such as fuschia, hot pink and orange shout exotic (yet global) style. Roughly woven, 'nubbly' cottons and hand-embroidered velvets, trimmings and tassels allude to authentic techniques and charming idiosyncrasies. Material gains are also high with once-worn wonders exuding frayed-around-the-edges appeal, such as an antique kimono patchwork quilt (fabulous on a utilitarian bed). As fashion statements that can be changed according to season or mood and lend themselves to bespoke tailoring, fabrics enfold a home with warmth and character.

Clockwise from top left:
A bedcover of antique *obis* and African-inspired cushion covers (Link Home) in Stanley Tan's home; Indian floor cushions are coordinated with a German sofa and rug in this passionate lounge off Johnny Tan's bedroom (Cynosure Design); lustrous silk and cotton saris (Little India and Arab Street, Singapore) look stunning draped over Balinese mango wood wall hangers or strung across open doorways, as at the Asmara Tropical and Asmara Ria Spas, Bintan Island, Indonesia.

Clockwise from right: Fusion food (by executive chef Tony Khoo of Sheraton Towers, Singapore) and flatware (Link Home) in Stanley Tan's dining pavilion; traditionally used for snacks, these pumpkin-shaped lacquered bowls *(bu)* from Myanmar look superb in a modern setting (Catherine LaJeunesse); elegant flatware (Link Home) and Cambodian silver (Judy McGrath); leaf-tied linen (Catherine LaJeunesse); Peranakan sweets made from tapioca flour and glutinous rice.

New Asian Entertaining

Central to Asian culture, where well-being is equated with eating, food is steeped in symbolism and ceremony. Presentation is often paramount, as in the *kim chi* cuisine of Korea or *kaiseki* of Japan, *yum cha* of Southern China or *salak* (carved fruit and vegetables) of Thailand. Table settings – traditional and contemporary – are art forms. New Asian entertaining is as simple as slipping a symbolic gift such as a fan or flower beside each place mat or as complex as setting aside a separate pavilion for dining. Where food is prepared is also increasingly important. Traditionally utilitarian and hidden, Asian kitchens are following global trends and becoming central living spaces (underlined by loft living in urban areas). Warm wood and stone surfaces are paired with industrial-chic stainless steel and its finger-proof counterpart, aluminium. Eastern nuances are subtle: a rice cooker or wok beside the coffee-maker; chopsticks or Oriental porcelain teamed with Western silverware; a spice rack or freshly grown herbs enriching one's culinary repertoire.

Clockwise from top: Mixed blessings. Laotian silk place mats and napkins (from Sandra Yuck of Caruso Designs, Vientiane), flatware from Bali and Burmese lacquered horsehair bowls; juxtaposing tropical fruits with modern glassware, such as this plate by Potterhaus Singapore, makes a striking table centrepiece; a lacquered sake set (Claire Chiang); a coffee table designed and hand-painted with Chinese motifs by Arabella Richardson is as refreshing as the iced water on it.

This page, clockwise from right: A slate feature wall in the outdoor bathroom of Sim Boon Yang's shophouse is traced with fossilized leaves; blue and white ginger jars from Shanghai (Callie Peet); a Chinese water jar in a miniature water garden (Chris White); an inventive way of using blue and white china (Catherine LaJeunesse); a mask-like pottery figure from Yogjakarta, Indonesia brings humour to a tropical garden (Claire Chiang).

Opposite, clockwise from top left: Jarring effect. Two antique water jars 'float' on an antique piece of timber in a Chan Soo Khian-designed home; a ceramic ginger jar holds cotton balls in Callie Peet's bathroom; a rare Neolithic pottery jar (Janet Stride); originally used to hold perfume or holy water, small ceramic pots from Thailand and Vietnam (Janet Stride); 19th-century blue and white china plates, salvaged from a shipwreck, support 18th-century ceramic figures used by Chinese painters to dilute ink (Ernesto Bedmar).

Down to Earth

Ceramics and earthenware, crafted from clay or mud which is then permanently hardened by heat, stone and related products are integral to modern Asian-style homes. Accents include coarse Indonesian stone mortars or smooth Thai sandstone sculptures used as candle bases, colourful Chinese *kamcheng* (lidded) storage jars, Thai celadon (great for tableware and lampbases) and thin-on-the-ground Neolithic (mainly Chinese) or prehistoric (often Thai) pottery. Prized in China, Japan and Thailand for more than 1,000 years, blue and white china is now so available worldwide that contemporary versions can be used every day – from the bathroom to the dining room. Architectural details slated to be big include broken-stone feature walls (indoors and out), terrazzo (this time from Vietnam), cool polished concrete floors and modern interpretations of Japanese gravel gardens.

Acknowledgements

Asmara Tropical Spa
Mayang Sari, Nirwana Gardens
Bintan Utara, Riau 291152
Indonesia
Tel: (62) 770 692 565
Email: asmara-spas@pacific.net.sg

Banyan Tree Gallery
Wah Chang House
211 Upper Bukit Timah Road
Singapore 588182
Tel: (65) 849 5888
Fax: (65) 462 4883

Bedmar & Shi Designers
12A Keong Saik Road
Singapore 089119
Tel: (65) 227 7117
Fax: (65) 227 7695
Email: bedmar.shi@pacific.net.sg

Blue Canopy
391 Orchard Road
#02-12G Ngee Ann City
Takashimaya
Singapore 238872
Tel: (65) 734 3505
Fax: (65) 734 5819

CK Collection
586 Serangoon Road
Singapore 218200
Tel: (65) 293 2301
Fax: (65) 291 7846
Email: ckcollection@yahoo.com

Club 21 Gallery
Four Seasons,
190 Orchard Boulevard
#01-07/8 Four Seasons Hotel
Singapore 248646
Tel: (65) 887 5451
Fax: (65) 735 2993

Cynosure Design Associates
400A East Coast Road
Singapore 428996
Tel: (65) 342 1200
Fax: (65) 342 1500
Email: cyno2000@singnet.com.sg

David's Antiques
58 Somme Road
Singapore 207875
Tel: (65) 291 8227

eco-id Architects
11 Stamford Road
#04-06 Capitol Building
Singapore 178884
Tel: (65) 337 5119
Fax: (65) 337 1563
Email: ecoid@pacific.net.sg

Far East Orchid
555 Thomson Road
Singapore 298140
Tel: (65) 251 5151
Fax: (65) 252 9318

Guan Antiques
31 Kampong Bahru Road
Singapore 169353
Tel: (65) 226 2281

Guz Wilkinson Architects
14B Murray Terrace
Singapore 079525
Tel: (65) 224 2182
Fax: (65) 224 1196
Email: guz@guzarchitects.com

Hassan's Carpets
19 Tanglin Road #03-01/06
Tanglin Shopping Centre
Singapore 247909
Tel: (65) 737 5626
Fax: (65) 235 4968

House of Huanghuali
69/70 Mohamed Sultan Road
Singapore 239006
Tel: (65) 235 6509
Fax: (65) 733 8655

Irene Lim & Associates
22 Sunset Heights
Singapore 597408
Tel: (65) 468 0822
Fax: (65) 463 0491
Email: minlin@cyberway.com.sg

Isabel Mendezona
109 Holland Road
Singapore 278552
Email: megabru@singnet.com.sg

Janet McGlennon Interiors
129 Devonshire Road
Singapore 239886
Tel: (65) 733 5580
Fax: (65) 733 5117
Email: janetmc@singnet.com.sg

Jim Thompson
390 Orchard Road
#08-04 Palais Renaissance
Singapore 238871
Tel: (65) 323 4800
Fax: (65) 323 5317
Email: siamsilk@singnet.com.sg

John Erdos Gallery
83 Kim Yam Road
Singapore 239378
Tel: (65) 735 3307
Fax: (65) 735 6901

Josephine Marais Flowers
611 Bukit Timah Road
Singapore 269712
Tel: (65) 469 7665
Fax: (65) 469 3874

Just Anthony
379 Upper Paya Lebar Road
Singapore 534972
Tel: (65) 283 4782
Fax: (65) 284 7439

Kerry Hill Architects
29 Cantonment Road
Singapore 089746
Tel: (65) 323 5400
Fax: (65) 323 5411
Email: khasing@singnet.com.sg

LaJeunesse Asian Art
94 Club St
Singapore 069462
Tel: (65) 224 7975
Fax: (65) 224 0475
Email:
lajeune@lajeunesseasianart.com

The Lifeshop
#04-30 Paragon
Singapore 238859
Tel: (65) 732 1719
Fax: (65) 732 1769

Lifestorey
3 Temasek Boulevard
#01-22/24 Suntec City Mall
Singapore 038983
Tel: (65) 336 0933
Fax: (65) 336 8381

The Link Home
#01-10 Palais Renaissance
390 Orchard Road
Singapore 238871
Tel: (65) 737 1503
Fax: (65) 733 7251

Mara Miri
65 Spottiswoode Park Road
Singapore 088654
Tel: (65) 225 6544
Fax: (65) 225 2918
Email: gnrptltd@singnet.com.sg

Pacific Nature Landscapes
Plot 2, 15 Joan Road
Singapore 298899
Tel: (65) 252 2136
Fax: (65) 251 1970

Pagoda House Gallery
125 Tanglin Road
Tudor Court
Singapore 247921
Tel/fax: (65) 732 2177

Poole Associates
Bungalow 3, Wee Nam Road
Singapore 307525
Tel: (65) 536 3928
Fax: (65) 356 9218
Email: poole@pacific.net.sg

Potterhaus Singapore
c/- Natif Glass Pte Ltd
238 Thomson Road
#03-21 Novena Square
Singapore 307683
Tel: (65) 255 7796
Fax: (65) 255 6642

Princess & The Pea
129 Devonshire Road
Singapore 239886
Tel: (65) 275 6345
Fax: (65) 736 3698
Email: pandp@singnet.com.sg

Roger's Carved Furniture
Blk 78 Guan Chuan Street
#01-41 Singapore 160078
Tel: (65) 224 3880

SCDA Architects
10 Teck Lim Road
Singapore 088386
Tel: (65) 324 5458
Fax: (65) 324 5450
Email: scda@cyberway.com.sg

Sensual Living
501 Orchard Road
#02-21 Wheelock Place
Singapore 238880
Tel: (65) 733 9656
Fax: (65) 733 7957
Email: sensual_living@pacific.net.sg

Sheraton Towers Singapore
39 Scotts Road
Singapore 228230
Tel: (65) 737 6888
Fax: (65) 737 1072

The Shophouse
22 Lock Road
Singapore 108939
Tel: (65) 344 0100
Fax: (65) 344 5509
Email: enquiry@theshophouse.com

**Stephen Caffyn Landscape
  Design**
14B Murray Terrace
Singapore 079525
Tel/fax: (65) 227 7152
Email: scld@land-arch.net

Studio 78
5 Canterbury Road
Alexandra Park
Singapore 119800
Tel: (65) 472 7238
Fax: (65) 274 2334
Email: s78@pacific.net.sg

Tantrum Interiors International
26 Tanjong Pagar Road
Singapore 088449
Tel: (65) 372 2108
Fax: (65) 324 0388
Email: tantrum.int@attglobal.net

Tarahome
583 Orchard Road
B1-06 Forum The Shopping Mall
Singapore 238884
Tel: (65) 238 6166
Fax: (65) 238 6066
Email: tarahome@jaygee.com.sg

**Tong Mern Sern Antiques,
  Arts and Crafts**
51 Craig Road
Singapore 089689
Tel: (65) 223 1037

Vanilla Design
137 Neil Road
Singapore 088866
Tel: (65) 324 6206
Fax: (65) 324 6207
Email: vanilladesign@pacific.net.sg

White Associates
#04-02 Blk 14 Leedon Heights
Singapore 267936
Tel: (65) 465 0219
Fax: (65) 465 7830
Email: chris@hpp-one.com

PT Wijaya Tribwana International
Villa Bebek
Jl. Pengembak No. 9B Mertasari
Sanur 80228, Bali
Indonesia
Tel: (62) 361 287668
Fax: (62) 361 286731
Email: ptwijaya@dps.mega.net.id

Wimberly Allison Tong & Goo
15 Scotts Road
#03-09/10 Thong Teck Building
Singapore 228218
Tel: (65) 227 2618
Fax: (65) 227 0650
Email: cettensperger@watg.com

Window to the Past
60B Martin Road
#04-06 Trademart (S) Pte Ltd
Singapore 239067
Tel: (65) 235 2760
Fax: (65) 734 3327

Woodsville Florist
139 Joo Chiat Place
Singapore 427869
Tel: (65) 345 2203
Fax: (65) 345 2790

X-tra Living
9 Penang Road
#01-01 Park Mall
Singapore 238459
Tel: (65) 336 0688
Fax: (65) 334 0688

Thanks also to all the people who
kindly allowed us into their homes
during the production of this book.